Advance Praise for Hiring Talent

As we enter the Human Age we have come to know that access to talent has surpassed access to capital as an employer's biggest challenge. Tom Foster gives us the steps needed to meet this challenge and bring the best on board in *Hiring Talent.*

-Thomas H. Shea, CEO
Florida/Caribbean, Right Management

Based my 37 years of business experience and employing thousands of individuals, the process outlined in this book will most definitely build the strongest most stable organizational structure you can find.

– Joe Seta
Seta Corporation
Direct-to-consumer catalogues

Tom Foster's guide to interviewing completely changed our hiring process. We hire more qualified candidates, and our turnover has been dramatically reduced. We have saved thousands of dollars in recruiting fees and rehiring costs for management since implementing his techniques. They work!

– Kristi Mollis, President
Everglades University

Using the Hiring Talent format, gives me far more confidence in my hiring decision and have discovered I actually enjoy many parts of the hiring process rather than just wanting to get it over with. It provides much greater clarity for expectations in the role and gives the applicant a much better understanding of the job.

– Blake Bennett, President
Bennett Marine
Worldwide supplier to the marine market

I just read the first part and decided to write a role description for a senior manager we are seeking to hire. I have always really been bad at this – but following your process, I was able write an organized role description that will really help us select the right person. Tomorrow I am going to read the next part and write the interview questions. This is incredibly useful.

-Catherine Colan Muth, CEO
OR Colan Associates
Experts in right-of-way and relocation services

Hiring Talent

Decoding Levels of Work
In the Behavioral Interview

Hiring Talent
Decoding Levels of Work in the Behavioral Interview

Copyright ©2013 Tom Foster

ISBN: Softcover - 978-0-9889165-1-7
ISBN: Digital Edition - 978-0-9889165-0-0

This book is designed to provide accurate and authoritative information related to the subject matter. It is sold with the understanding that the publisher is not engaged in rendering legal, accounting or other professional services. If you require legal advice or other expert advice, seek the services of a competent professional.

Printed in the United States of America

All trademarks are the property of the respective company.

Dedication

This book is dedicated to Charles "Red" Scott. In 1995, he purchased TEC Florida and before the ink was dry, I was the first person he hired. He asked me if I felt like I was lucky. He also reminded me that, despite his name, the richest bloodline has always been and will always be burnt orange.

Acknowledgments

I would like to thank Barry Shamis for instilling in me, the discipline of asking prepared questions. His potent teaching related to behavioral interviewing was my first glimpse into the power of this process.

Elliott Jaques (1917-2003) compiled the most amazing research on levels of work and capability. Elliott provides the science underneath the hiring decision.

Kathryn Cason was my inspiration to stay close to the bounds of Elliott's research, not to overthink things, to recognize the elegant simplicity of time-span.

Stephen Clement, who stood next to Elliott during his years with the US Army and at CRA Mining in Australia, helped me focus on the work. "It's all about the work."

Jerry Boyle of Pinpoint Profiles taught me about the two big lies.

I would like to thank all of my Vistage/TEC members who allowed me access to their internal thinking and their organizations to practice in.

Special mention goes to those who rendered invaluable feedback on how this book was put together, Dr. Arthur Keiser, Mitch Talenfeld, Blake Bennett, Chris Clement, Linda Carroll, Bill Kent, Ian Sabal.

Table of Contents

Prologue – The Two Big Lies

In the unfamiliar conference room, Ryan was nervous. He was early for his interview. Alone, he could smell the fresh polish on his shoes. His untouched coffee grew cold. The door swung wide, and in walked Drew, the hiring manager.

Drew was cordial enough, but distracted. He was in the middle of a meeting when Ryan's arrival was announced. He had planned to prepare better for this interview, but time got away from him.

"Thanks for coming in," Drew began, glancing over the resume. "We could use someone with your talents."

Ryan's professional resume was impressive. It was mostly true, with only minor exaggeration. Drew glanced at his watch, wondering how long this would take. He was really busy this morning.

Ryan had practiced for this interview with a professional headhunter, so he was ready for the first three questions, verbatim from his role-play sessions. He had printed out and studied the company website, so he made it sound like he already worked there.

Reading off the resume, Drew leaned forward. "Your last job is almost exactly like the opening we have here. I'm not making an offer, but when would you be available to start?"

Ten minutes and two questions later, Drew was nodding, "Ryan, what do you say, let's take a quick tour of the facility?"

"Okay," Ryan replied, scratching his head.

It was a quick tour. Drew figured luck was on his side to find someone so early in the interview process.

Ryan was a little surprised at the size of the machines on the shop floor. They were bigger than they looked in the pictures on the internet. But, he kept smiling. And it was loud. Someone from the floor asked a question that he hardly understood, but the smile on his face covered his absence of understanding.

"What do you think?" Drew shouted over the noise. "I know we are a smaller operation than your last job, but you can handle this, right? And do you really think you could start on Monday?"

Ryan drew in a deep breath, preparing to tell the two big lies, "Yes, I can," and "Yes, I will."

The Problem

Hiring managers do not interview candidates often enough to get good at it, are seldom trained to conduct effective interviews and rely on faulty assumptions throughout the entire process. Most managers are totally unprepared. They ask the wrong questions and allow stereotypes to get in the way. They end up making a decision within the first three minutes of the interview, based on misinterpretations and incomplete data.

One of the most important functions of management is to build the team. If this job is done well, life as a manager will be wonderful. If this job is done poorly, life will be miserable, for a very long time.

Why This Book is Different

This is the only book on hiring that blends the research on levels of work[i] with the discipline of behavioral interviewing. The research on levels of work, pioneered by the late Elliott Jaques, is powerful science. The discipline of behavioral interviewing is the most effective method for its application. This is the only book that puts these two ideas together in a practical framework for managers faced with the hiring decision.

The Framework

There are several steps in the hiring process. This book will focus on the four most important parts –

- Identify the level of work in the role
- Organize the role description
- Create a bank of interview questions
- Conduct the face-to-face interview

If the manager gets these four steps right, the rest falls into place. If the manager gets these four steps wrong, the rest doesn't matter.

All the Steps

Here is the long list of steps, including the big four.

- Evaluate the necessity for the position
- **Identify the level of work (Part I)**
- **Organize the role description (Part II)**
- Write the job posting
- **Create a list of interview questions (Part III)**
- Source candidates
- Resume intake and sorting
- Telephone screens
- Telephone interview (including Skype)
- **Conduct the face-to-face interview (Part IV)**
- Permissions and releases
- Behavioral assessments
- Background checks
- Reference checks
- Drug screen
- Selection process
- Make the offer
- Orientation
- Training
- Evaluation period

Here is a Preview

Part I – Set the Foundation.

This is the cornerstone. First, identify the participants in this process. Second, identify the level of work in the role. Level of work is likely a new concept for most managers. Inside every task, there is a level of decision making, a level of problem solving. I will show you how to identify the level of work and how to measure it.

Part II – Organize the role description.

I will show you an easy way to capture critical role requirements using a specific template that supports this process.

Part III – Creating questions about future behavior.

I will demonstrate how to painlessly create a bank of sixty written prepared questions, specifically related to the role. I will give you a step-by-step method to construct effective questions that get to the point, and how to avoid those questions that waste your time.

Part IV – Conduct the face-to-face interview.

For every prepared question you ask, I will train you to ask two additional drill-down questions. I will show you how to ask for the specific data you need to make a better hiring decision.

Part V – Details, details.

At the end, I will fill in the details and leave you with some parting thoughts.

Part I – Set the Foundation

The Players

There are very specific roles for people to play in the process of Hiring Talent. Most of these roles are unspoken, assumed, vague and undefined. And that's where the trouble begins. There are very specific roles, very specific accountabilities and very specific collaboration that must take place. Here are the players

- Manager-once-removed (MOR)
- Hiring manager
- Interview team members
- Human Resource manager

During this recruiting period, both the manager-once-removed and the hiring manager have to hang their day-to-day activities on a coat hook and focus on the hiring decision.

Manager-Once-Removed

The manager-once-removed (MOR) is the hiring manager's manager. The MOR is the driver in the hiring process.

Most companies mistakenly believe in the ability of the hiring manager to make an effective decision without coaching and support. Most hiring disappointments can be avoided by understanding the required role of the manager-once-removed.

Organizational Chart
Manager-Once-Removed
Hiring Manager
Open Role

What is a Manager Accountable For?

A manager is that person in the organization held accountable for the output of other people. This simple statement carries great weight. Many managers assume, when an employee makes a mistake, that the employee is accountable for the mistake. Alternatively, I assume the employee is doing their best, and it is their manager that I hold accountable for the mistake. In most companies, accountability is placed one layer too low and the manager is off the hook. A manager is that person in the organization held accountable for the output of other people.

In Hiring Talent, there is a selection decision about to be made by the hiring manager. This decision could be a great decision or a poor decision. Who should be held accountable for the quality of this decision?

I assume that the hiring manager is doing their best, bringing full attention and discretionary judgment to this decision. It is the hiring manager's manager, the manager-once-removed (MOR) that I hold accountable for the quality of the decision made by the hiring manager.

Without help or coaching, most hiring managers flounder in this process and in the end make a poor decision. That help and coaching comes from the manager-once-removed.

I feel the push-back from MORs, who tell me they do not have time to participate in this process, but I stand my ground. It is the MOR that I hold accountable for the quality of the decision made by the hiring manager. I expect the MOR to be the leader in this decision. I expect the MOR to –

- Evaluate the necessity of the open role
- Properly identify the level of work
- Insist on and participate in the drafting of the role description
- Insist on and participate in the creation of a bank of interview questions
- Lay the ground rules for conducting the interviews
- Coach the hiring manager through the selection decision

I hold the MOR accountable for the quality of the decision made by the hiring manager. This accountability creates high levels of collaboration between the MOR, the hiring manager and other interview team members. The MOR is not off the hook.

I get resistance from MORs who tell me they are too busy to read resumes and make screening phone calls. My response is, "What is more important than to build the infrastructure of your team? The reason you are so busy, with your management and motivation issues, is that you may not have done a good job of this, in the first place."

I expect the MOR to drive this process, qualify the slate of candidates, bring discipline to each step and make sure the decision made by the hiring manager produces the best person from the candidate pool.

Why not just have the MOR make the hiring decision? It is a fair question, but the answer has to do with accountability. When the successful candidate becomes a team member, completing task assignments, doing their best, it is the hiring manager that is accountable for their output. The MOR develops the slate of qualified candidates, but it is the hiring manager who makes the hiring decision. At a minimum, the hiring manager has veto authority over the final selection.

Hiring Manager

The hiring manager makes the final decision, and lives with the consequences of that decision. I expect the hiring manager to –

- Provide input related to the necessity of the open role.
- Provide input in identifying the level of work in the role.
- Participate in the drafting of the role description.
- Participate in the creation of a bank of appropriate interview questions.
- Follow the ground rules set by the MOR for conducting the interviews.
- Exercise their best judgment in making the selection decision.

Interview Team

Most companies, these days, create interview teams, to put extra eyes in the process. The participation of interview teams can be very effective *or* can turn the process into chaos. Participants on the interview team must be chosen with purpose and given specific assignments in the process. Technical specialists on the interview team can bring great value by asking questions about technical skills.

While the interview team is a team, I expect each member to play one at a time. Some companies conduct 2-on-1 or 3-on-1 interviews. More than one interviewer in the room puts artificial pressure on the candidate and may spoil candid (truthful) responses. My preference is to have one interviewer at a time, with one candidate in the room. Occasionally, I will allow an observer, maybe two, but only one interviewer.

The MOR orchestrates the participation of interview team members, creates clear criteria for questions, coaches on interview behavior and insists on discipline in the process.

These instructions are not very effective. "Hey, do you have a minute to go talk to this candidate? Everyone else likes him. Go see if you like him, too?"

Interview team members, in separate interviews, may ask overlapping questions. It might be valuable to debrief candidate responses to the same question from two different interviewers. It might also be valuable to have one interview team member focus on a specific area outside the expertise of other interview team members.

Human Resource Manager

Many companies assume that the Human Resource Department should handle all aspects of recruiting, including the final selection. But, the Human Resource manager cannot be held accountable for the direct output of the new employee on the production line, so, in the end, the Human Resource manager cannot be the hiring manager. The Human Resource manager, however, can play a very valuable role related to the discipline in this process.

In the role of a technical contributor, the Human Resource manager can work with the MOR and assist in the identification of the level of work in the role. The HR manager can insist on step completion in each stage of the process. If the hiring manager wants to skip the step of writing the role description, the HR manager, as an auditor in the hiring process, can stop or delay the process until the role description has, indeed, been written. The HR manager can facilitate effective meetings to create the bank of interview questions and ensure collaboration between the manager-once-removed (MOR), the hiring manager and other members of the interview team.

The role of the Human Resource manager, as the process auditor and facilitator can be very helpful, increasing the effectiveness of the selection decision.

Managers Are Mostly Unprepared

Managers are mostly unprepared and candidates have been professionally coached.

Unprepared, most managers (MORs and hiring managers) begin the interview process down two strikes. Most managers avoid the real work required, and then improvise from there. They often hire the person they like, rather than the person most qualified.

Why? – Because they failed to define the critical requirements in the role.

Managers Don't Practice

Hiring managers don't interview candidates often enough to get good at it, are seldom trained to conduct effective interviews and rely on faulty assumptions throughout the entire process. The candidates they face have been coached by headhunters, trained through role play, and are intent on beating the manager in a game of cat and mouse.

Managers Miss Clues

Often, hiring managers miss critical clues from candidates during the interview. The clues are there. Why does the interviewer miss them? Most managers enter the interview room hopelessly unprepared. Interview team members get drawn into the process impromptu, with little advance notice. They don't stand a chance of finding out even the most basic data about the candidate.

Managers Harbor Stereotypes

The candidate sports a visible tattoo and the hiring manager reaches into the back of the brain to surface a stereotype about people who wear tattoos. Conclusions are immediately drawn, a hiring decision reached in seconds, and the interview hasn't even started. Why do hiring managers make decisions based on stereotypes and bias? (Tattoos are only the beginning).

First Impressions

When I speak with managers, they tell me that, in the end, most hiring decisions are made during the first few minutes of the interview. When I press for details, the decision is made on some vague first impression, a feeling about the candidate. Why do hiring managers make the decision so quickly? Too quickly? Why does intuition play such a large role in the hiring decision?

Intuition can lead to important lines of questions, but it can lead to the wrong conclusion, if those questions are not asked.

Manager Loses Control of the Interview

Sometimes I sit in on interviews. It is like watching a game of tennis, seeing who is in control. It is amazing how candidates are more skilled at controlling the interview than the hiring manager. Why do managers lose control?

Asks the Wrong Questions

The pain is often excruciating, listening to questions interviewers ask. Why did you ask that? What were you thinking with that question? I thought I had a favorite ineffective question, but it has recently been replaced, "If you were an animal, what would you be?"

Most managers arrive at the interview, unprepared. They make the hiring decision in the first few minutes, based on a first impression, a stereotype, a bias. They bumble their way through the interview, often losing control, asking the wrong questions.

There is a Solution

Hiring Talent is based on simple principles within the capability of every manager. There is a logical sequence and some diligent work.

Here is the first insight. Managers are people. They are subject to their first impressions. They carry stereotypes and have gut reactions to other people. That's fine, that's not the problem. The problem is that managers do not have a method to collect the data they need to offset those first impressions. They do not have a method to capture the critical data, related to the role that helps them make better hiring decisions.

Don't Change Who You Are

I am not going to change you, as a person. I will not tell you to deny your intuition. I will give you a method to put the right data on the table so you can do a better job of getting to know the person who shows up in the role.

In Spite of Your First Impression

I do not care if you harbor a stereotype about a person with a tattoo. If you follow the method in Hiring Talent, you will finish the interview with 180 pieces of data to balance that stereotype and you will make a better hiring decision in spite of your first impression.

Who the Hell is Elliott Jaques?

This is the chapter title in a book by Jerry Harvey,[ii] who introduced me to a powerful body of research compiled over a period of fifty years by the late Dr. Elliott Jaques. Much of the practice in Hiring Talent is based on this specific research. Elliott Jaques is likely the least known management scientist on the planet, yet his narrative on levels of work creates a useful platform for the hiring process.

While few people know about Jaques' research, he wrote 23 books on the subjects of organizational structure, accountability and authority, managerial and cross-functional working relationships. His most famous books are *Requisite Organization* [iii]and *Social Power and the CEO*.[iv]

Resting on the foundation of Jaques research, Hiring Talent is focused on its practical application in the behavioral interview.

Levels of Work

The biggest mistake most managers make is underestimating the level of work in the role.

Inside every task, there is a level of decision making and a level of problem solving. That level can be identified and measured. Before the right person can be selected for the role, the manager has to understand the level of work. Examine this list of construction tasks for a door and trim contractor.

1. Before noon today, measure and hang the door, nail the trim wood around the door.

2. Over the next four months, coordinate the measuring of the openings, the ordering of all the doors, the hanging of the doors, including the trim wood around all the doors and windows (60 doors, 120 windows) in this building as it is constructed.

3. Over the next year, create a system to estimate, schedule, order and stock the doors and trim wood required for all the projects (175 projects), receiving the stock only as needed for each project, but so we never run out.

Each of these task assignments requires a different level of decision making and problem solving. The level of work can be identified and measured.

Identifying the Level of Work

To identify the level of work in the list of tasks above, there are three sets of clues.

- Decisions. What are the decisions that have to be made, to effectively complete the task prior to the deadline?
- Problem solving. What are the problems that have to be solved, to effectively complete the task prior to the deadline?
- Time-span of the task. What is the length of time established to complete the task?

Decoding these clues is the first step to understanding the level of work. Identifying the level of work is the first step in Hiring Talent.

Level V Roles
Level IV Roles
Level III Roles
Level II Roles
Level I Roles

Why is Time-span Important?

What separates one person's ability to perform, from another? That is the central question in every interview. Paying close attention to the level of work in the role and matching a person's capability to do that work, can dramatically improve hiring decisions. Decision making and problem solving are clues, but Jaques found the key metric in measuring level of work was time-span.

Time-span is the length of time a person can effectively work, without direction, into the future, using their own discretionary judgment, to achieve a specific goal.

Take a deep breath and re-read the definition, because time-span capability is the critical difference between each candidate.

Drew's New Hire

Drew was beside himself. "I don't know why Ryan can't handle this job. We asked him all the questions in the interview. We were quite thorough. He knows the name of each piece of equipment. He can tell you exactly what it is used for and how it is used. To run the equipment, we even have trained technicians for him to manage."

"What's the problem?" I asked.

"All he has to do is keep the equipment busy. We have sales orders from the front office. All he has to do is look at the sales orders, translate those into work orders, make sure we have the right materials in stock and schedule the work on each machine."

"And?" I pressed.

"And that's where he stops. He can keep one or two machines busy, but we have fifteen machines and plenty of work for all of them."

"Who was the supervisor before Ryan got hired?"

"Oh, he was a good guy, kept the place humming. Got promoted to our other plant in Michigan," Drew explained.

"And there was no one else on the production crew that could take over?"

"No, a good technician doesn't necessarily make for a good supervisor. It's one thing to push out today's work. Totally different to make sure all the machines are scheduled for each shift for the next three weeks. Lots of moving parts."

"Can't you train someone?" I probed.

"It's not a matter of training," Drew shook his head. "Some people have it and some people don't."

"So, what is it, that some people have and others don't?" I wanted to know.

Capability is the Key

Each person is different. Each person has their own natural capability, embedded in their DNA. Fixed at birth, capability naturally grows as a person matures.

Given a task, a person applies their natural capability, along with skills and their interest in the work, to complete the task. Applied capability can be seen because there is a work product. A manager can see a person's applied capability by observing their work output.

It is the responsibility of every manager to determine the level of work in the open role and evaluate the candidate's time-span capability for that level of work. Matching the level of work in the role to the current capability of the candidate is the key to Hiring Talent.

Level I Roles

Level I roles are populated by technicians, equipment operators, clerical workers and data entry operators. The work product in Level I roles typically consists of *individual output.* The output from a Level I role is often the direct product or service experienced by the customer. Team members in Level I roles receive task assignments from a supervisor, coordinator or designated manager.

Claude's Team

I was talking with Claude, a supervisor, about his team. "Those two over there, are the new guys, one has been here a month, the other just got out of orientation last week. They are learning, but it will take them a while to catch on to how we do things around here."

"How often do you have to check up on them?" I asked.

"In the morning, we go over the work orders from the production schedules. A little huddle meeting. I check back in about 15 minutes to make sure they are moving in the right direction. Then, they're good for a couple of hours. Right now, I am not as worried about their production output, as much as doing the work correctly."

"And the rest of your team?"

"The rest of the crew has been here at least a year, some, four or five years. They know what to do. For them, our morning huddle is as much social, as it is to look at production for the day. I walk the floor a couple of times, morning and afternoon, just to see if they have questions, admire some of their handiwork."

"When they run into a problem, how do they solve it?" I pressed.

"There are some things they can try, but if they can't figure it out pretty quickly, they either come to Tony, or me?" Claude replied.

"Tony?"

"Tony is the team leader. Sharp kid. Only been here two years, great technician, twenty-eight years old."

"So, how does Tony solve problems?" I was curious.

"Same as the other guys, but he is quick. If one solution doesn't work, he has something else to try. If that doesn't work, he tries something else. Boom, boom, boom, problem is usually solved. When I have to be out of the office, or on vacation, Tony is my assistant. I can leave him in charge, and not worry. But Tony won't be with us much longer."

"Why's that?"

"I was talking with my manager. She has had her eye on Tony since the beginning, thinks he is ready for supervisor training."

Decisions Made, Problems Solved

Most discretionary decisions in Level I roles revolve around pace and quality.

"Am I working fast enough to complete the assigned task in the time expected? Am I working carefully enough to meet the quality standard set for this task?"

Attention to quality standards translate into quality as a value-add at Level I. While companies may create those standards at Level III or Level IV, the delivery of quality standards into the product or service often rests in the hands of those in Level I roles.

Team members in Level I roles may work in the same room with other people, but are rarely concerned with other teammates' activities unless there are direct hand-offs of work tasks, one to another.

Work materials and equipment are organized only for the working session. Ordering and coordinating additional work materials for future work, next week, next month, is generally outside the bounds of Level I.

Time-span (1 day – 3 months)

Level I task assignments are generally expected to be completed within one day or a few days. Experienced team members may be expected to continue projects without supervision as long as a month. The most experienced team members in Level I roles may informally assist other team members in trial and error troubleshooting, demonstrate work routines or special skills and may be assigned projects as long as three months in length. Some organizations may call these most-experienced Level I roles *team leaders*. Team leaders may have no managerial authority but may assist their managers in task assignments between Level I and Level II roles.

Level I			
Longest Time-span Goals	**Tools**	**Problem Solving**	**Value**
1 Day-3 Months	Real tools, equipment, machinery	Trial and Error	Quality

Level II Roles

Level II roles are populated by supervisors, coordinators, first line managers and project managers.

Decisions Made, Problems Solved

The problems solved and decisions made are longer in time-span, than Level I roles.

Claude's Role

"So, your manager is sending Tony for supervisor training. What's different about a supervisor's role?"

"Well, since I am a supervisor, I can tell you first hand," Claude continued. "Each guy on the crew is focused on their individual task assignment. As a supervisor, I have to be focused on the whole team, how everybody and everything works together."

"You said Tony was pretty good at trouble-shooting. I assume you're pretty good at solving problems yourself?"

"I have a secret," Claude chuckled. "When these guys run up against a problem, they think it's the first time it has ever happened, so they try this or that to figure it out. You know, trial and error. Truth is, the problems our customers have, we have likely seen before. We document our 'best practice' solution to those problems in our SOP manual. For the most part, when I see a problem, I just have to identify its elements and look it up. Looking up the answer in the back of the book is a lot easier than starting from scratch. It's all about experience, tapping into that experience to solve problems."

"Kind of like watching a YouTube video on how to fix something," I smiled. "So, how do you keep everything straight?" I asked.

"At first, I tried to keep it in my head. Big mistake. Soon, I figured out some checklists we could use for different projects, so we wouldn't forget stuff. It makes a big difference when there are twenty-five things to remember. And schedules, I use a master schedule to coordinate people, materials and equipment, all in the right place, at the right time. The master schedule is one of my primary tools. With that, I can tell you what every day should look like for the next four weeks."

"So, you have to be able to look ahead for the next four weeks?"

"Oh, longer than that," Claude snapped back. "When I meet with my manager, we talk about things much further out. We have a seasonal business, so our workforce grows and shrinks each year. We can use a little overtime as a buffer, but I actually have a workforce plan that goes out one year. Recruiting and training doesn't happen overnight. We have to know when to begin hiring and when we have to move people around as the workload goes down. With the workforce plan, it's pretty predictable."

Team Coordination

Level II roles are concerned with the coordination of production with people, materials and equipment. It is a team orientation rather than an individual orientation.

Level II roles are accountable for materials in the current working session, as well as the ordering of future materials, for next week, next month. Level II roles may provide input on min/max quantities set by their manager.

To be effective, the tools in Level II roles consist of schedules, checklists and short meetings directly related to production or operational output.

Time-span (3 – 12 months)

Experienced Level II roles may be responsible for projects and operations three to six months in the future. The most experienced in Level II roles may be expected to work on projects up to 12 months in length.

Level II			
Longest Time-span Goals	Tools	Problem Solving	Value
3-12 Months	Schedules, checklists, meetings	Experience, manuals, best practices	Accurate, complete, on time.

Level III Roles

Level III roles are populated by managers responsible for production consistency, to create predictability in work output. Their focus is on the creation, monitoring and improvement of systems. A system is a series of steps in a specific sequence that creates a predictable output.

Rachel's System

"I am not an industrial engineer," Rachel started, "but I know how to design a system. We are a large fast-food restaurant chain and each of our work cells is a small system. Cooking French fries is done according to a system, a series of steps in a specific sequence.

- Frozen potato slices are poured from a bag into a metal basket.
- The metal basket is submerged in cooking oil at a specific temperature.
- An automatic clock is tripped when the metal basket is submerged.
- The automatic clock rings an alert when the correct time has elapsed.
- The metal basket is removed from the cooking oil and set to drain for a specific period of time.
- The French fries are poured from the metal basket onto a heat tray ready for bagging.
- Salt is applied to French fries.
- French fries are bagged, to order, for the customer.

"When you watch it from the front of the store," Rachel continued, "it looks simple, but it took a full year to figure out all the elements, to fabricate the right basket and a timing system that could stand the heat near the fryer. Even the placement of the drain racking to minimize work steps had to be analyzed."

"What problems did you have to solve?" I asked.

"Oh, the problems were real," Rachel replied. "Why were the fries overcooked? How does cooking oil get splashed on the floor? Why are the fries oily?"

"So, you had to try some different things?" I quizzed, trying to sound smart.

"Well, trial and error sometimes works, but sometimes the solution requires analysis. When the fries were overcooked, it had nothing to do with the cooking time. Turns out, the cooking time was calibrated for frozen sliced potatoes. If the potatoes were allowed to thaw, they came out crunchy instead of crispy. It's a small thing, but the frozen state of the potato had to become part of the system."

"How about the cooking oil on the floor?" I wanted to know.

"That was a strange problem, because it didn't happen all the time. Just sometimes, there would be this unexplained cooking oil on the floor. We checked for leaks, but that wasn't it. We had to step back and examine the sequence. Sometimes, and only sometimes, the cook would put the fry basket empty into the cooking oil, then pour frozen potatoes directly into the cooking oil. A little dramatic, but there would be a flash boil that splashed grease onto the floor.

So, the specific sequence of steps had to become part of the system. Put the potatoes in the basket, first."

"I have to close the loop on this," I said. "Sometimes the fries were oily?"

"It's the drain step. Fries only need to drain 20-30 seconds, but if the cook was in a hurry and bagged the fries immediately, they were greasy. We decided not to put a timer on that part of the system, it was more of a training problem. But that training step became part of the system.

"So, now you know, next time your fries are overcooked, it's a system problem."

Decisions Made, Problems Solved

Level III roles create sustainable efficiencies. The problems solved are related to work flow, system layout and sequence. Given a problem, the Level III manager examines the system. Designing, maintaining and troubleshooting systems may require root cause analysis or comparative analysis.

Time-span (1 – 2 years)

The time-span of the longest projects at Level III typically range from 1-2 years. To manage projects of this length, Level III roles depend on planning scenarios, employing "what if" analysis. In pursuit of any task assignment, they create alternate paths to the goal and contingency planning to anticipate roadblocks outside their direct control.

Here is another example of a Level III project with a time-span greater than one year, the installation of new piece of heavy, expensive capital equipment on a plant floor. Here is the system sequence.

- Evaluate the necessity for the capital equipment.
- Determine the current manual work cells that will be replaced by this equipment.
- Gather and evaluate proposals from different manufacturers.
- Reference-check current customers of this equipment from each manufacturer.
- Select a manufacturer.
- Negotiate the terms of the contract and delivery.
- Schedule the delivery.
- Lay out the plant floor to accommodate the new equipment.
- Construct a temporary work-around for the current manual work cells to be displaced by the new equipment.
- Jackhammer and reinforce the concrete floor to handle the weight of the new, heavy equipment.
- Take delivery of the new equipment.
- Install the new equipment.
- Troubleshoot why the new equipment doesn't work (new equipment never works).
- Fly in a team of engineers to get the new equipment working.
- Train personnel to operate the new equipment.
- Do first-piece inspections from the new equipment.

- Transition output from the manual work cells to be replaced by output from the new equipment.
- Discontinue output from the manual work cells, replace with total output from the new equipment.
- Ramp output from the new equipment to new, higher, output capacity.

Time-span of the task - 12 months.

Level III			
Longest Time-span Goals	**Tools**	**Problem Solving**	**Value**
1-2 Years	Flow charts, sequence, planning	Root cause analysis, comparative analysis	Single system efficiency, consistency, predictability

Level IV Roles

As organizations grow, they develop more systems and subsystems. Level IV roles are typically responsible to integrate these multiple systems together. But, this is not a multi-tasking role. Level IV managers must understand the dependencies, inter-dependencies, contingencies and bottlenecks that exist between multiple systems. The goal is to integrate these systems and sub-systems together into a "whole system."

Decisions Made, Problems Solved

Level IV managers (typically a VP, COO, Director of Operations) have larger picture decisions to make.

- How does one system impact another system?
- Is it okay for one system to go idle while other systems catch up?
- Where is the constraint in overall throughput?

The focus in problem solving often requires the Level IV manager to step out of the internal focus of a single system to examine the output of multiple systems interacting with each other. This may involve the momentum of a *reinforcing* system offset by the impact of a *balancing* system.[v]

Sales, as a *reinforcing* system, are often offset by the capacity of operations, as a *balancing* system. Unrestrained sales that outstrip operational fulfillment create backorders and unhappy customers. Unrestrained operations that outstrip sales create inventory overstocks, carrying costs and cash flow issues. Matching sales (*reinforcing* system) with operational fulfillment (*balancing* system) creates a "whole system" optimized for organizational output.

Time-span (2-5 years)

Problem solving at Level IV is generally related to longer term initiatives which may take 2-5 years to achieve. Task assignments at Level IV are defined by operational planning and longer term strategic planning.

Level IV			
Longest Time-span Goals	**Tools**	**Problem Solving**	**Value**
2-5 Years	System metrics	Systems Analysis	Multi-system efficiency, "whole system" throughput

Level V Roles

Level V roles are populated by business unit presidents and small company CEOs. Their attention must be broad, accounting for the organization's strategic vision against the realities of the market.

Decisions Made, Problems Solved

These are often the only roles in the organization with the authority to make decisions about long term commitments of resources for facilities, capital equipment, including the collateralization of lines of credit. Level V roles use financial metrics and models to make long term decisions and commitments to ensure that the organization stays relevant and viable in the marketplace.

Time-span (5-10 years)

The long term view at this level ranges from five to ten years. These roles watch long term market trends, think about mergers and acquisitions, geographic expansion and product line extensions. They position resources and take long term risk.

Levels of Work			
Longest Time-span Goals	**Tools**	**Problem Solving**	**Value**
V 5-10 Years	Financial models, market studies	External Analysis	Value in the marketplace
IV 2-5 Years	System metrics	Systems Analysis	Multi-system efficiency, throughput
III 1-2 Years	Flow charts, sequence, planning	Root cause analysis, comparative analysis	Single system efficiency, consistency, predictability
II 3-12 Months	Schedules, checklists, meetings	Experience, manuals, best practices	Accurate, complete, on time
I 1 Day-3 Months	Real tools, equipment	Trial and Error	Quality

Levels of Work in Different Disciplines

Examples of level of work in physical trades, construction and manufacturing are easiest to identify. Other disciplines, including service work and knowledge work can also be calibrated by identifying decisions made, problems solved and the length of the longest time-span task in the role.

Managerial Roles

Level I – Time-span (1 day – 3 months)

There are no managerial roles at Level I. The work in most Level I roles is described as individual direct output.

Level II – Time-span (3 – 12 months)

Coordinators, supervisors, project managers, first line managers, assistant managers all populate Level II roles. The purpose of these roles is to make sure the production work at Level I is completed on time and within the specifications of the output.

Level III – Time-span (1 – 2 years)

Managers at Level III are accountable for the creation of sustainable production systems. These systems must be constructed to anticipate fluctuations in production volume as well as variance in materials, equipment, and customer specifications.

Level IV – Time-span (2-5 years)

Managers at Level IV are accountable for multi-system and sub-system integration. Problem solving at this level is more complex, troubleshooting a system problem that may actually be caused by its interaction with another system inside or outside the organization.

Level V – Time-span (5-10 years)

The managerial role at Level V is most often the business unit president. This role is typically the only role that can make signature commitments to building leases, long term capital equipment, lines of credit, mergers and acquisitions. The business unit president must ensure that the strategy of the organization is relevant to the market it serves. In the following discussion of individual business models, each model will typically have a business unit president or chief executive.

Level VI – Time-span (10-20 years)

This role emerges as an organization grows to hold multiple business units in its portfolio. Much of the work at this level is to make decisions about the long term viability and growth of its individual business units. Capital investment, return on equity and market opportunity make up the day-to-day issues in this role.

Accounting Roles

Level I – Time-span (1 day – 3 months)

Accounts Payable, Accounts Receivable and other clerical roles are typically high Level I roles. Much of this work is transaction based, including computer data entry and reconciliation routines.

Level II – Time-span (3 – 12 months)

Accounting roles at Level II typically require the compilation of source data for activities like payroll reporting, quarterly payroll reconciliations and insurance census reporting.

Level III – Time-span (1 – 2 years)

Accounting system Level III work is typified by full charge bookkeeping, trial balance proofing, monthly, quarterly and annual financial statement reporting. Even though some reporting appears to be monthly or quarterly, these Level III roles simultaneously consider the impact of those monthly and quarterly numbers on the annual compilations, extending the time-span of the task to one year.

High Level III roles are populated by controllers, which would include project accounting or job cost accounting where accounting periods may extend beyond a single fiscal year.

Level IV – Time-span (2 – 5 years)

Accounting roles at Level IV, like CFO roles, require the anticipation of fiscal events more than two years out. This would include negotiation for and maintenance of lines of credit, covenant reporting to banks and market trend analysis that impacts cash requirements. In an integrator role, the CFO inspects system metrics to evaluate the performance of multiple systems working together for total organizational financial performance.

Engineering Roles

Level I – Time-span (1 day – 3 months)

There are few engineering roles at Level I. Internships and other learning roles in engineering require high Level I, in some cases, Level II capability.

Level II – Time-span (3 – 12 months)

Most engineering production work is completed at Level II. In many cases, these roles are non-managerial, individual technical contributors. This would include engineering output in the form of CAD/CAM, blueprints and other engineering drawings. This work consists of selecting and compiling project elements in a technical drawing or technical model.

Outside of drawing work, Level II roles would be populated by sustaining engineers, manufacturing engineers, production engineers, whose work would include engineering problem solving in a production environment where problems require more than trial and error solutions, adhering to standardized practices create at Level III.

Level III – Time-span (1 – 2 years)

Some engineering work is system specific, requiring higher levels of capability. Here, there are specialized hydraulic, mechanical, chemical and electrical engineers. The work at this level is more complex than bringing known elements into a drawing. This design work involves problem solving of unknown elements inside an unknown system. The task assignment may be to create a machine, tool or system that functions within a specified tolerance according to an engineering discipline. This role may be non-managerial, as an individual technical contributor, or managerial coordinating the output of Level II engineers.

Level IV – Time-span (2-5 years)

Engineering work at this level would involve the integration of multiple disciplines. Some engineering problems require the integration of hydraulic, mechanical, chemical and electrical disciplines. This role may be non-managerial, as an individual technical contributor, but more likely will be managerial, coordinating the output of Level III engineers.

Computer Programming Roles

Level I – Time-span (1 day – 3 months)

There are few computer programming roles at Level I outside of interns or learning roles.

Level II – Time-span (3 – 12 months)

Computer programming at Level II involves the creation of functional routines or small applications that perform simple calculations or queries. Coding work at Level II would most likely be under the direct supervision of a programming manager.

Level III – Time-span (1 – 2 years)

Programming work at Level III would include the creation of full system applications or an application module. Level III roles may delegate some of the coding activity to Level II under programming guidelines and specifications created at Level III.

Level IV – Time-span (2-5 years)

Programming work at Level IV would include the integration of full system applications into enterprise systems, containing multiple modules. Much of the coding work would be completed at Level II and Level III under the direction and guidance of Level IV roles.

Sales Roles

Level I – Time-span (1 day – 3 months)

The level of work in sales roles can be calibrated by inspecting the length of the sales cycle. Short sales cycles can be effectively maintained by trained order takers. Level I sales roles can be found in catalogue call centers, counter sales and sales oriented customer service centers.

Level II – Time-span (3 – 12 months)

Sales work at Level II is found in longer sales cycle projects, where building relationships is important. This sales work consists of prospecting for new customers, qualifying prospective customers, gathering customer needs according to a checklist, matching products to customer needs, making presentations, negotiating and closing the sale. On the customer side, the counterpart to Level II sales work would be the purchasing agent.

Level III – Time-span (1 – 2 years)

Decisions in business to business purchases often require additional input. While the buying criteria for most purchasing agents is price, the Level III buyer, sometimes a specifying engineer, is more concerned about function. Interacting with a Level III buyer may require the capability of a Level III sales person, a product engineer. Sales work at this level is more concerned with needs analysis, product match and application. Sales functions like prospecting may be delegated to sales team members at Level II.

Level IV – Time-span (2-5 years)

Occasionally the buying decision involves product functionality that integrates with other systems that exist in the customer organization. The Level II purchasing agent is concerned about price. The Level III specifying engineer is concerned about function. The Level IV buyer is concerned about how the product or service will integrate with other systems in the company. Sales cycles greater than two years may require Level IV capability to understand the complexities of how the product or service integrates into customer systems. A primary accountability for this level of work in the selling company will be feedback loops into research and product or service development. Examples of Level IV sales roles exist in pharmaceuticals, automobile components, electronic components, large scale construction projects, international logistics, financial instruments and insurance products.

Restaurant Business Models

Level I – Time-span (1 day – 3 months)

Cooks, servers, greeters and bartenders make up Level I roles in this business model. Individual direct output describes the work.

This industry has created stop-gap roles at Level I, which appear to be managerial, such as shift supervisor and manager of the day (MOD). Close inspection of the time-span in these roles is required to determine if the decisions are stop-gap at Level I or managerial at Level II. Stop-gap decisions are temporary decisions made in the absence of a manager. The stop-gap authority of a shift supervisor or manager of the day (MOD) is limited to low risk decisions within the level of work in the role.

Level II – Time-span (3 – 12 months)

The manager in a single store restaurant is often a Level II role. The work is intense, but the time-span of tasks like recruiting and food purchasing fall within a one-year time frame. A store manager in a multi-store restaurant chain follows system specifications and direction from roles at Level III or Level IV.

Level III – Time-span (1 – 2 years)

In a single store restaurant, this role is often the owner, who had a great idea for a restaurant. This level of work includes restaurant theme, menu creation, commitment of resources to multi-year leases.

Manager roles in upscale and large multi-store restaurants may require Level III work. A chef's role in an upscale restaurant involves much more than cooking, in the creation of food themes, recipes, hardware inventory, capital equipment purchases and kitchen workflow. Level III roles would include workforce planning, training programs and store profitability.

Level IV – Time-span (2-5 years)

This level of work in the restaurant business model is mostly found in multi-store operations. Contracts with food purveyors include details that integrate into the systems at each of the store locations with budget items for advertising, media buys and branding. Capital requirements extend beyond operational expenses into real estate investment, expansion and franchise agreements.

Fleet Service Business Models

Level I – Time-span (1 day – 3 months)

Service technicians populate Level I roles in this service model, extending to dispatch operators and customer service personnel. Many fleet service models are based on simple service functions with perceived complexity or requiring specialized equipment. This includes plumbing, air conditioning and carpet cleaning technicians.

Level II – Time-span (3 – 12 months)

Fleet service technicians in Level I roles require coordination and scheduling functions contained in Level II roles. Supervisors and manager-of-the-day (MOD) roles ensure that service delivery will meet standards, be complete and on-time.

Level III – Time-span (1 – 2 years)

To be efficient in its service delivery, fleet service companies employ managers to create, monitor and improve systems. Recruiting and training to these systems are necessary to establish branded processes in these moderate to high turnover businesses. Fleet service models spawn franchise operations. Franchisees purchase proven Level III systems from franchisors, reducing the number of roles needed at Level III in franchise stores.

Level IV – Time-span (2-5 years)

Multi-store operations may require capability at Level IV as issues of fleet leasing, volume equipment purchases, uniform contracts, legal exposure and insurance become more complex with a larger employee base.

Creative Agency Business Models

Level I – Time-span (1 day – 3 months)

This business model includes advertising agencies and media production companies. In addition to Level I clerical roles, many creative roles are found at Level I, including graphic artists, layout designers and production technicians. Much of their work consists of task assignments assigned by Level II or Level III project managers or department managers.

Level II – Time-span (3 – 12 months)

Project coordinator or project manager roles organize project work into discrete task assignments, ensuring compliance with project specifications, meeting customer approvals and project deadlines. These roles interface in working relationships with account managers also at Level II. Account management maintains the working relationship with the customer, looking at longer time-span tasks related to overall campaign work or project initiatives.

Level III - Time-span (1 - 2 years)

To be efficient and profitable, agencies and media companies must develop systems so that creative work can be organized within budgets on a repeated basis. The output at Level III would include work flow charts, step-by-step quality approvals and media specification standards, all to ensure that the creative work is consistent in its quality and that first time customers become repeat customers. Effectiveness at Level III can be seen by those agencies who have a stable client base with little turnover.

Level IV - Time-span (2-5 years)

Level IV expertise is required by larger agencies and media companies involved in cross platform media buys, integrated lead generation systems and where fast-response systems must be constructed and integrated. Level IV roles may be involved in the acquisition and deployment of software to create customized cross-platform media pieces based on database variables generated in real time. The observed work output may occur in real time, but the acquisition and deployment of those systems may take more than two years to become reliably productive.

Financial Planning Service Models

Level I - Time-span (1 day - 3 months)

Financial service models, like financial planning, involve work roles across all levels. Most Level I work is clerical in nature. Because of the risk and legal exposure, much of this clerical work is boilerplate, using templates created at Level III and Level IV.

Level II – Time-span (3 – 12 months)

A large part of financial planning service models is in sales and customer relationship building. Entry level sales roles involve Level II work following checklists and compiling customer data in relatively simple financial programs and products.

Level III – Time-span (1 – 2 years)

As customer requirements become more complex, the work requires analysis and the ability to project further into the future. More complex financial products are not suitable for all customers, requiring additional analysis from roles at Level III. These Level III roles may still be involved in direct sales efforts, but with additional qualifying steps to identify the more complex customer.

Level IV – Time-span (2-5 years)

Financial service sales at Level IV are more technical in nature, looking at issues larger than principal preservation and growth. There may be tax implications, inheritance issues, gifting issues, generation skipping, estate and trust work. While the mechanics of these issues may be delegated to Level III or Level II roles, the customer relationship and strategy requires capability at Level IV.

Insurance Agency Business Models

Level I – Time-span (1 day – 3 months)

Like financial services work, insurance agency models require clerical work, much of which is boilerplate and pro-forma.

Level II – Time-span (3 – 12 months)

Level II roles in this model would include entry level sales personnel, involved in the sale of standard insurance products. While the products are standard, significant compilation of customer data is required to qualify the customer and determine rate information. This customer data must be complete, accurate and within specific time deadlines to comply with renewal periods.

The backside of insurance product sales requires Level II roles involved in marketing those qualified customers to underwriters, maintaining underwriting relationships and adjusting policy parameters to fit the customer needs. Claims management is also populated by Level II roles to ensure that claims are documented to standard and filed appropriately.

Level III – Time-span (1 – 2 years)

Some customer insurance requirements are more complex, requiring risk management analysis supported by insurance products. Sales roles at Level III must have the ability to analyze customer systems for risk, determine exposure bases and execute mitigating programs like safety training to impact risk exposure.

Level IV – Time-span (2-5 years)

Large customers may require integrated risk management solutions that require Level IV roles to assess and manage large risk pools. This may involve specialized re-insurance resources, self-insurance entities and legal corporate structures to protect assets. Sales roles at Level IV are looking for complex customers with complex risk management issues.

Construction Trades

Level I – Time-span (1 day – 3 months)

Construction trades have a wide range of Level I roles, from direct laborers to team leaders. Direct laborers work on time-span tasks from one day to one week. The most experienced laborer on a work crew may have a designated role as team leader. Team leader work remains at Level I, where this person may answer questions, model the correct work method, but without the responsibility of assigning tasks to other crew members. On occasion, a team leader may assist a supervisor or foreman, but is not accountable for scheduling, re-scheduling or authorizing overtime.

Level II – Time-span (3 – 12 months)

Level II roles would be populated by supervisors and foreman. Accountability would include the coordination and scheduling of personnel, equipment and materials. On a job site, they likely retain the highest decision making authority. This role often has wide latitude in day-to-day decision making within limits set by their manager. At a project level, they have non-managerial working relationships with project managers.

Project management is typically a Level II role, focused on planning and project administration. Project managers have non-managerial working relationships with superintendents, construction managers, supervisors and foremen.

Level III – Time-span (1 – 2 years)

Level III roles include construction managers and superintendents. They often have accountability over several job sites, responsible for master scheduling, work force loading and large equipment mobilization. Construction managers have non-managerial working relationships with project managers.

There are project manager roles at Level III, sometimes designated as senior project manager. This level of work is distinguished by project time-spans exceeding one year, but, less than two years in length.

Level IV – Time-span (2-5 years)

Level IV roles include C-level, Chief Operating Officers and Vice-Presidents. These roles may not be required for small sub-contractors, but are necessary in large organizations, prime contractors and general contractors. Large projects that extend beyond two years require management capability to coordinate multiple sub-contractors, complex project tracking and project budgets.

Legal Business Models

Level I – Time-span (1 day – 3 months)

With the advent of computers and electronic communication, the need for clerical roles in legal firms has diminished, but there are still large amounts of paper documents that must be created, copied and filed.

Level II – Time-span (3 – 12 months)

Roles at Level II include para-professionals, research assistants and junior attorneys. They compile the legal elements that make up real estate contracts, supporting documentation, business contracts and routine agreements. In simple matters, they operate independently. In complex projects, they operate under the direction of another attorney or specialist.

Level III – Time-span (1 – 2 years)

Most legal work is performed by attorneys in roles at Level III. While many tasks appear to be short in time-span, the impact of a decision, contract or agreement may extend well into the future.

Level IV – Time-span (2-5 years)

Legal work seems important, because its impact is long-lasting. Lease agreements may last five years. Settlement agreements may last a lifetime. The longer the impact of a legal agreement on an individual or company, the greater the uncertainty. Negotiating and writing a settlement agreement requires the imagination to predict relevant events in the future that might have impact on the parties involved. Legal roles at Level IV include senior attorneys and specialists.

Public Accounting Business Models

Level I – Time-span (1 day – 3 months)

Like legal work, Level I roles in public accounting firms have been minimized by computerization. Computer systems have replaced manual systems. Computerized bookkeeping systems have migrated from the public accounting firm to the offices of their clients. Payroll returns are no longer prepared by the accounting firm, but by large payroll processing companies. Even receptionists have been largely replaced by voicemail. Clerical roles at Level I have not disappeared, but many of those desks are now empty.

Level II – Time-span (3 – 12 months)

Computers have had an impact on Level II and Level III work as well. Because most accounting work is governed by a complex set of rules and guidelines, computer software has been written to remove much of the decision making surrounding the treatment of an accounting or tax issue. Level III or Level IV decision making has been replaced by computer software operated by accounting roles at Level II.

A client may be greeted by and have coffee with the senior partner in the public accounting firm, but the work is compiled by an accountant in a Level II role.

Level III – Time-span (1 – 2 years)

Computers do not make decisions, they do not reason, but follow precise rules created by the software programmer. While most accounting and tax issues are strictly governed by rules, there are many areas where judgment is required. An accountant in a Level III role may consider several ways for a company to account for depreciated equipment or to handle its inventory method. Decisions must account for company objectives related to cash flow or tax treatment. These decisions cannot be made by a computer, but require analysis and judgment at Level III.

Level IV – Time-span (2-5 years)

While computer software can accurately calculate tax returns, there are some accounting issues that require judgment on issues that extend beyond two years. Accounting roles at Level IV would be involved in decisions surrounding trusts, estates, separating or merging corporate entities. The role may still be called accountant, but the capability required for this work extends from two to five years.

Medical Business Models

Level I – Time-span (1 day – 3 months)

Technology has helped create many Level I roles in the medical industry. Sophisticated medical machines require technicians and operators. Nursing assistants can handle many of the routine tasks that formerly required higher level skills and experience.

Computers have created the ability to record volumes of patient medical data. Many administrative roles are now required to record medical conditions and test results into computer software.

Level II – Time-span (3 – 12 months)

The difference between a nursing assistant in a Level I role and a registered nurse in a Level II role is in the decisions that are made. A nursing assistant at Level I is accountable for administering drugs according to the specification on a patient chart. A registered nurse in a Level II role is more likely to catch the mistake of a drug label attached to the wrong patient chart. It is not just a matter of more experience or training, but a higher level of judgment in making decisions.

The emerging role of the physician assistant at Level II, in the delivery of medical services, will be interesting to watch as technology allows for remote supervision by Level III and Level IV physicians.

Level III – Time-span (1 – 2 years)

Level III medical roles are populated by general physicians, internists and some specialists. The time-span of the patient's disease would indicate the level of work required in the physician role.

Level IV – Time-span (2-5 years)

Long term diseases may require the physician, specialist or surgeon to integrate research, complex symptoms and patient response to treatment. Disease management across populations for the practical elimination of polio, tuberculosis and smallpox likely required Level IV roles. Future disease management for cancer, diabetes and immune disorders will require roles matched to the time-span of those conditions.

Education Models (K-12)

Level I – Time-span (1 day – 3 months)

Clues to the level of work in roles for education, both public and private, can be seen in student-teacher interaction combined with lesson planning. Most Level I teaching is performed by student teachers and teacher's aides. Often, they will be assigned to work one-on-one or with very small groups to achieve learning objectives. Lesson planning is short term or non-existent. Most often, Level I teaching is closely supervised by other teachers at Level II or Level III.

Level II – Time-span (3 – 12 months)

Most classroom teaching roles are at Level II. Lesson planning is mandated by administration and usually extends only to the end of the scholastic term. Learning methodology is primarily the presentation of reading material or other media about a defined subject area, accompanied by a test for comprehension.

Math skills begin with kinesthetic manipulation of objects and progress to memorization of addition and multiplication tables.

Level III – Time-span (1 – 2 years)

The difference between a Level II classroom teacher and a Level III classroom teacher may first be observed in their lesson planning. The output of Level III planning extends beyond the mandated scholastic term to full year or multi-year outcomes. Level III teaching roles sit on curriculum committees and contribute to the long term culture of the school environment.

Level III roles are also populated by principals at smaller schools. Accountable for the smooth operation of smaller schools, these principals must design the system in which each school operates in concert with teachers, students and parents.

Level IV – Time-span (2-5 years)

Larger schools are more complex, with bigger student populations, more teachers, higher public visibility, more internal and external programs. The level of work in the role of the principal moves to Level IV. It is likely that this principal sits on school district policy committees, manages a complex budget and directs the day-to-day operation with the help of an assistant principal at Level III.

It's All About the Work

The biggest mistake most managers make is underestimating the level of work in the role. Identifying the level of work is the key to effective hiring decisions. Failing to accurately identify the level of work will guarantee hiring the wrong person. Matching the level of work with the capability of the candidate is the first requirement in the selection process. It is one of four absolutes.

The Four Absolutes

With the level of work identified, the focus shifts to find the most effective candidate. According to Jaques, in the hiring process, there are four key elements to be discovered about each candidate.

1. Capability – matched to the level of work in the open role.
2. Skill – technical knowledge and practice related to the open role.
3. Interest, passion – value for the work in the open role.
4. Reasonable behavior – connected to the open role.

These are absolutes. Any one of these four elements can disqualify the candidate.

Four Absolutes for Effectiveness	
Capability	Skill
Interest Passion	Reasonable Behavior

Capability - How Big Is the Role?

Most discussions of capability use analogies and imprecise descriptions.

- How big is the role?
- How heavy is the role?
- How much horsepower does this role require?

These descriptions make for colorful conversation, but are not helpful to specifically define and measure capability required in the role.

Connecting Time-span with Capability

Decisions and problem solving are clues to level of work, but the most accurate measure of level of work is time-span. This definition is worth repeating.

> Time-span is the length of time a person can effectively work, without direction, into the future, using their own discretionary judgment, to achieve a specific goal.

It's All About the Work

Armed with the level of work, the interviewer only has to learn if any of the candidate's former roles match the level of work required in the open role? How effective was their decision making? How effective was their problem solving? How effective was the candidate in that level of work?

With an understanding of levels of work, these are the two central questions.

- What is the level of work in the open role?
- Does the applied capability of the person match the level of work?

Skill

The second absolute for success, in any role, is skill. The candidate may have the capability to handle the level of work in the role, but if they do not possess the specific skills required, the manager may not see that capability.

A skill can be learned, and contains two elements, technical knowledge and practice.

If the skill is to throw a ball, there is some technical knowledge required. Does the ball have seams? Is the ball round or oblong? Are fingers placed around the ball, or inside the ball? Is the ball thrown underhand or overhand? What sport is the ball used in?

But, technical knowledge has little bearing on the success at executing the skill. Much may be known about the ball, but to master execution, practice is required. Skill requires both technical knowledge and practice.

Interest, Passion (Value for the Work)

A candidate may have the capability and they may have the skill, but it matters little if there is no interest or passion for the work. If a person places a high value on the work, they are likely to have interest or passion for the work. If a person places a low value on the work, they are likely not to be interested.

Reasonable Behavior

Reasonable behavior sounds unremarkable, but, as one of the four absolutes, it can derail a candidate's effectiveness. Reasonable behavior has two parts, one positive, one with a dark side.

- Habits
- Absence of an extreme negative temperament

Habits

There are habits which contribute to success and habits that get in the way. If timeliness is a critical role requirement, then showing up early might be a positive habit, showing up late, a negative habit. Often, ingrained habits have a profound impact on effectiveness.

Absence of an Extreme Negative Temperament

This is the dark side of reasonable behavior. Jaques described this dark side as minus "T".

The "T" stands for temperament. Related to temperament, Jaques was mainly concerned only with the extreme negative temperament or minus "T," the baggage that some people carry that gets in the way of their effectiveness. This is conduct clearly outside the bounds of reasonable behavior.

Minus "T"

Here is a short list of behaviors in the category of minus "T."

- Arrogant
- Self-Absorbed
- Perfectionist
- Micro-manager
- Defensive
- Control Freak
- Stubborn
- Pig Headed
- Abrasive
- Rude

So, reasonable behavior is required, positive habits that contribute to effectiveness, and the absence of Minus "T."

Most Interviews are Too Narrow

Unfortunately, most interviews are solely conducted for technical knowledge, one small slice of the four absolutes. If a candidate scores well on technical knowledge, wild assumptions get made about the other absolutes. To make an effective candidate selection, interview questions must be crafted for all four elements.

Most Hiring Processes are Too Loose

Most companies have a very loose process for hiring. They solicit resumes, schedule some interviews and then pick somebody.

Hiring Talent is serious business. Look at the annual compensation package, then double or triple that amount to figure what a poor hire will cost the company in terms of wasted compensation, re-work and overwork on the part of others covering for the poor hire. Look at the impact on morale and unproductive management time.

Hiring Talent requires discipline in a core set of specifically defined steps.

- Organize the role description
- Create a bank of interview questions
- Conduct an effective face-to-face interview

Each step in the hiring process exists for a very specific reason.

Part II – The Role Description

It's All About the Work

Organizing the role description is the cornerstone of the hiring process. Do this step well and everything else flows. Do this step poorly and you get a big mess. Here are the elements organized into a template. Below the template is an explanation of each element.

Role Description Template
Title
Purpose
Level of Work
Manager and manager-once-removed
Key Result Area #1
- Tasks and Activities
- Accountability

Key Result Area #2
- Tasks and Activities
- Accountability

Key Result Area #3
- Tasks and Activities
- Accountability

Key Result Area #4
- Tasks and Activities
- Accountability

Key Result Area #5
- Tasks and Activities
- Accountability

Key Result Area #6
- Tasks and Activities
- Accountability

For an electronic version of this template, visit www.hiringtalent.com.

Role Title

The title is only a short hand reference for the role. Be aware that many business models use the same role titles to create entirely different expectations. Here are some examples.

Level I - Technician, laborer, machine operator, clerk.
Level II - Supervisor, coordinator, director, project manager, engineer.
Level III - Plant manager, department manager.
Level IV - Vice-President, COO, CFO, unit manager.
Level V - CEO, business unit president.

And there are hundreds more. Use role titles that are meaningful in your industry, in your company.

Purpose

This is a single sentence that specifically explains why this role exists.

Example – Role – Floor Supervisor
The purpose of this role is to ensure that all materials, personnel and equipment are scheduled to meet the daily, weekly and monthly production requirements dictated by the target production output list.

Level of Work

This is one element of the template where the judgment of the manager-once-removed is most important. Judging the level of work will depend on the decisions to be made, problems to be solved and the time-span of the longest task in the role. Every role will contain many tasks with different target completion times. Identifying the level of work will depend on the longest time-span task in the role. If the candidate has difficulty with the longest time-span task, it is likely they will underperform in the role.

Manager and Manager-Once-Removed (MOR)

This element of the role description names the team member's manager and the manager-once-removed (MOR), so there is no ambiguity about which manager is held accountable for the output of the team member, where task assignments originate, and where to go for help.

Key Result Areas (KRAs)

This is the structure for the role description. Key Result Areas (KRAs) group similar tasks and accountabilities together so they make sense. KRAs create an organized structure for the design of the work in the role.

Example – Role – Floor Supervisor

Key Result Areas
- Raw Material Inventory
- Personnel Scheduling
- Equipment Scheduling
- Production Output
- Production Reporting
- Equipment Maintenance
- Personnel and Recruiting
- Professional Development

Tasks and Activities

Inside each Key Result Area (KRA), there are both general and specific descriptions of tasks and activities required to meet the accountability associated with the KRA.

Accountability (Goal)

As a result of the tasks and activities, there is an expected outcome, an accountability, a goal. In each KRA, what is the goal, a "what, by when?"

Example – Role – Floor Supervisor
Key Result Area – Production Output
    Accountability – Prior to the end of each month, the Floor Supervisor is accountable for the production of finished goods according to the target production output. (Time-span = 1 month)

Field Work

If you are using this book as a practical field guide, this is your opportunity to organize a role description, using the template provided, for a real role in your organization. This will be most helpful if your organization is currently recruiting for this role.

Your role description can be used through the rest of this guide in the following steps -
- Assembling a bank of interview questions
- Conducting the interview

If this step (organizing the role description) is done well, the rest of the steps in Hiring Talent fall into place. An example follows.

Role Title?

Floor Supervisor

Purpose for this role?

The purpose of this role is to ensure that all materials, personnel and equipment are scheduled to meet the daily, weekly and monthly production requirements dictated by the target production output list.

Level of Work

This is a Level II position. Longest time-span tasks range between 3-12 months.

Manager and Manager-Once-Removed (MOR)?

Manager – Plant Manager
MOR – VP of Operations

Key Result Areas for this role?

1. Raw Material Inventory
2. Personnel Scheduling
3. Equipment Scheduling
4. Production Output
5. Production Reporting
6. Equipment Maintenance
7. Professional Development

KRA #1, tasks, activities? Primary accountability?

Raw Material Inventory
The Floor Supervisor will maintain the raw material inventory required for the production of all finished goods according to the MIN/MAX schedule supplied by the plant manager. The Floor Supervisor will prepare purchase orders to replenish raw material stock to the MIN/MAX levels. The Floor Supervisor will coordinate the receiving and stocking of all raw materials to the designated bin locations. The Floor Supervisor will review production forecasts three months into the future for critical and long lead time raw materials.

Accountability - Prior to the end of each month, the Floor Supervisor will have successfully maintained raw material stock no less than 5 percent below the MIN level and no more than 10% above the MAX level during that month, and that during each rolling three month period, no production line was interrupted or stopped due to a raw material stock out. Time-span = 1 month.

KRA #2, tasks, activities? Primary accountability?

Personnel Scheduling
The Floor Supervisor will maintain all personnel production schedules for all machines and assembly operations, including the accommodation of all approved vacation and personal time requests. The Floor Supervisor will coordinate with the Plant Manager to assure personnel coverage without undue overtime.

Accountability - Prior to the end of each rolling four week period on Friday, the Floor Supervisor will post personnel production schedules on the production shift bulletin board. The Floor Supervisor will be accountable for production personnel scheduling so that no overtime is required, except for specific projects approved by the Plant Manager. Time-span = 1 month.

KRA #3, tasks, activities? Primary accountability?

Equipment Scheduling
The Floor Supervisor will schedule all machine time to accommodate the necessary production runs according to the production schedule published by the Plant Manager. This includes the re-scheduling of machines in the event of machine downtime to meet the production schedule.

Accountability - Prior to the end of each rolling four week period, on Thursday, the Floor Supervisor will post the machine time schedule on the production shift bulletin board. The Floor Supervisor will be accountable for monitoring machine uptime three times each day and on-call to ensure that machine rescheduling due to downtime conforms to the original production schedule published by the Plant Manager. Time-span = 1 month.

KRA #4, tasks, activities? Primary accountability?

Production Output
The Floor Supervisor will monitor all production line operations, fielding line problems and making coordination decisions.

Accountability - Prior to the end of each week, the Floor Supervisor will be accountable for meeting the production schedule assigned for that week by the Plant Manager. This output will be reviewed in a meeting with the Plant Manager on a weekly basis. Time-span = 1 week.

KRA #5, tasks, activities? Primary accountability?

Production Reporting
The Floor Supervisor will ensure that all finished goods coming off the line are properly inspected according to the QA standards and counted prior to boxing and staging for finished goods inventory.

Accountability - Prior to the end of each week, the Floor Supervisor will deliver to the Plant Manager finished goods counts, including quality discrepancies and reason codes. Prior to the end of each month, these finished goods counts will be reconciled with internal cycle counts of finished goods and be within .2 percent of book inventory. Time-span = 1 month.

KRA #6, tasks, activities? Primary accountability?

Equipment Maintenance
The Floor Supervisor will be responsible for all equipment maintenance and monitoring of long term overhaul processes.

Accountability - Prior to the end of each month, the Floor Supervisor will submit to the Plant Manager, a three month backward schedule of actual expenses for all equipment listed on the floor equipment manifest. For each piece of equipment listed, a three month backward maintenance log and a three month forward maintenance schedule will be submitted and reviewed with the Plant Manager. In addition, prior to the end of each year, the Floor Supervisor will publish a stage-of-life and end-of-life schedule for all equipment listed on the floor equipment manifest. This would include the scheduling of all major overhauls (requiring extended out of service) and retirement or exchanges for new equipment. Time-span = 12 months.

KRA #7, tasks, activities? Primary accountability?

Professional Development
The Floor Supervisor will engage in learning more about the technical processes associated with this role by reading relevant trade journals, participating in relevant association activities, and pursuing relevant certifications agreed to by the Floor Supervisor's manager and the manager-once-removed.

Accountability - Prior to the end of each year, the Floor Supervisor, the Floor Supervisor's manager and manager-once-removed will create a professional development document outlining agreed-to learning activities. This document will be reviewed on a quarterly basis to track relevant progress. Time-span = 12 months.

Part III – Creating Questions About Future Behavior

Creating Interview Questions

Most managers are totally unprepared to conduct an effective interview. They go up against candidates who have been coached, who stayed up late the night before, practicing their answers. Managers ask the wrong questions and allow stereotypes to get in the way. They end up making a decision within the first three minutes of the interview, based on misinterpretations and incomplete data.

Best Predictor of Future Behavior

The best predictor of future behavior is past behavior. That is the basis of the behavioral interview.

Some might question that philosophy. "Can't someone learn something new? What about change? Can't people change?"

People do learn, and people do change, but the best predictor of future behavior is past behavior. The behavioral interview collects specific data about past behavior related to the open role. This strict discipline avoids open-ended questions, future-based and hypothetical questions. It is counter to many popular and counterproductive approaches to the interview.

Open-ended questions allow the candidate to ramble, to make up responses they think the interviewer wants to hear. Open-ended responses require the interviewer to organize and interpret the meaning of the stories being told by the candidate.

In the interview, the intention is to cut through the stories and focus on specific behaviors related to the critical role requirements. The hiring decision is based on specific evidence collected during the interview. The best predictor of future behavior is past behavior.

Making the Wrong Decision

Why do managers, who are generally pretty smart and make reasonable decisions, suddenly go brain-dead when it comes to the selection process? Here are some reasons why.

Too Quick

Managers don't get enough practice at hiring. They do it only when someone quits (and they are never prepared), when someone is fired (and the replacement is never on board) or when production is suddenly busy and they need more help on the line.

For most managers, hiring is an annoyance, and the sooner they trudge through the process, the better. Managers have too many other important things to do, than conduct a bunch of interviews.

When I talk to managers, they tell me that they typically make their hiring decision within three minutes of the start of the interview.

Thumbs down, the manager may finish the interview, take the candidate on a tour of the company, but the decision was made during the first three minutes.

Thumbs up, the manager almost always says "they immediately knew," within the first three minutes. While intuition is important, making the decision without supporting data is dangerous.

Stereotypes and Bias

Humans hold stereotypes and bias about almost all of their experience. Stereotyping helps to survive in a complex world. Humans categorize experience so that they can quickly make sense of it. The problem is not stereotypes. The problem is, especially in the interview process, managers are not prepared to dig deep enough to find out the real truth about the candidate. Because they are not prepared, and because they make the decision too quickly, they have nothing else to go on except those stereotypes and bias.

Beating It Out of You

I am not going to beat stereotypes out of you. What I will do, is teach you to slow down and come to the table prepared. When managers arrive prepared, they will collect 180 pieces of data so they can make a better selection. Collecting this data will take longer than the first three minutes of the interview.

Ineffective Interview Questions

Even those who come prepared, typically ask the wrong questions. Here is my all-time favorite – least effective interview question.

"Where do you see yourself in five years?"

But, that question is on every interviewer's list. It is asked of most every candidate, in every interview ever conducted.

It is still a terrible question. Here's why. It is future-based, calls for speculation from the candidate, does not have to be true, and cannot be verified. Worse yet, the interviewer has to do something with their interpretation of the response. Future based questions encourage the candidate to guess what the interviewer wants to hear, encourages the candidate to make up stories, or outright lie.

Hypothetical Questions

"What would you do if?" It is a terrible question. Again, future-based questions call for speculation. Candidates, who have been coached, done research, read some trade journals, are likely to have close-enough textbook responses to sound authoritative. It does not mean they have ever actually solved that problem, made that decision or worked with that team. Hypothetical questions encourage candidates to make up stories and lie.

Open Ended Questions

This actually used to be the "prescription" for interview questions. Wrong. Open ended questions allow the candidate to babble, to talk about what *they* want to talk about. The interviewer does not have time for that. The interviewer needs to collect important critical data, related to the open role, so they can make a proper selection. The interviewer must set the agenda.

Leading Questions

"Do you think teamwork is important?" The right answer is embedded in the question. Leading questions train the candidate to look for answers in the question, rather than to tell the real story of their experience.

The intent of the question is valid, but the way the question is asked, destroys the truth in the response. Future planning and teamwork are valid behaviors, and may be critical role requirements. How can better questions be crafted?

Constructing the Question

If the best predictor of future behavior is past behavior, the interviewer only has to ask about specific past behavior related to the critical role requirements. This is the basis for the practice of behavioral interviewing.

Crafting the Question

- What is the critical role requirement?
- What behavior is that connected to?
- Ask about a time when?
- Ask about details?

Here is an example.

Critical Role Requirement

Ability to supervise five other people on a project team.

Behavior

Candidate has acted in a managerial capacity on a project or in a former role with approximately five team members.

Ask About a Time When?

Tell me about a time when you were the manager on a project?

Ask About Details

- How many people were on the team?
- What was your title (role), what was the managerial relationship?
- Was this team organized only for this project or did they work together all time?
- What was the purpose of the project?
- How was the project plan created?
- How long was the project?
- How did you, as the manager, create and assign tasks?
- How did you, as the manager, monitor progress on the project?

- How did you, as the manager, evaluate the effectiveness of each team member contributing to the project?
- What changes occurred during the course of the project?

Why These Questions Are Better

Why are these questions better than hypothetical or future-based questions?

- The responses are real.
- In addition to technical knowledge, the response can reveal how decisions were made and problems solved.
- Responses are verifiable. Hypothetical responses cannot be fact-checked, they never existed.
- Prevents lying. Repetitive details reduce exaggeration. Made-up stories disappear by the third example.
- The interviewer does not have to interpret what a response means. All the responses, based on the questions, should be simple facts that do not require interpretation.

My Favorite Questions [vi]

- Tell me about a time when?
- Step me through?

What Data is Needed to Make a Decision?

The cornerstone of this process rests in the research of Elliott Jaques, who provides guidance in his four absolutes for success.

Four Absolutes for Success

1. Capability (for the level of work)
2. Skills (technical knowledge, practice)
3. Interest, passion (value for the work)
4. Reasonable behavior (habits, absence of Minus T)

Constructing Questions for Capability

I often hear stories from managers, describing why a team member has just failed to perform. The stories almost always use an analogy to describe the failure.

- The person isn't big enough for the job.
- This person isn't the brightest light bulb in the box.
- This person just can't connect the dots.

These are all approximations for what Jaques called "capability." The analogies, above, tell the story, but are not very helpful when it comes to selecting talent.

Matching Level of Work

Capability is most reliably revealed by identifying the level of work in former roles and determining if that level of work matches the level of work in your open role. Level of work is most easily identified by looking at the decisions made, problems solved and the time-span of the longest tasks in the former role.

Less Complex or More Complex

The shorter the time-span of the task, the less likely its complexity, a lower level of work. The longer the time-span of the task, the more likely its complexity, a higher level of work.

Short Time-span Projects

For a short time-span project that is due tomorrow, it is likely known what materials are needed, the source for those materials, who will be assigned to the project and the specific steps to achieve the goal. At least, these elements should be known, the project is due tomorrow.

Longer Time-span Projects

For a longer time-span project, due in 18 months, many elements may not be known, some specifics may change. Material may be ordered late in the project, the source for those materials may not be known. Specific personnel assigned to this project may not be currently employed. And, the client may change their mind about all of this a dozen times before the project is completed. More uncertainty equals more complexity.

Longer Time-span Projects and Higher Capability

Jaques demonstrated, through validated studies, that longer time-span projects require higher capability, and that capability can be measured by identifying the time-span of the tasks or projects in the role. Questions must be constructed, not just for the content in the candidate's experience, the decisions made and problems solved, but also for the time-span of tasks and projects in former roles.

Constructing Questions for Skills

Every skill has two parts, technical knowledge and practice. While technical knowledge is important, it only reveals how much a person knows. In many ways, it is not important how much a person knows, more important what a candidate can do.

This example looks at the required skills for project estimator.

- Meet with clients to receive specifications (interpersonal skills)
- Review specifications for completeness and accuracy.
- Draw prints, blueprints, take-offs to visualize the scope of the project, materials and quantities.
- Translate specifications into a Bill of Materials or Buyout.
- Apply standards to the scope and quantities to estimate hours of labor.
- Draft a proposal using the drawings, quantities and hours.
- Meet with the client to review the proposal.

Each of these steps, in the project estimator role, requires some technical knowledge, easy to ask about. But, technical knowledge is only half the story. The other half is how the knowledge is applied and how the candidate practices those skills.

My Favorite Questions

Tell me about a project when?
Step me through the process?

Questions Related to Practice

- During this past year, how many projects did you estimate?
- Using your computer estimating system, tell me about the project that took the longest time to estimate?
- What were the factors that made that project take longer than other projects?
- Did you ever work on more than one project at the same time?
- What was the highest number of projects that you worked on at one time?
- Step me through how you managed that number of projects?

While it is important to understand the technical knowledge required in each step, these questions help the interviewer understand workload volume, the time-span of each step and handling simultaneous tasks.

Constructing Questions for Interest, Passion

The candidate may have the capability, with the necessary skill, but if the candidate is not interested in the work, does not value the work, it is likely they will not be successful in the role.

Values

What work is the candidate interested in? What value does the candidate place on the work? If they place a high value on the work, they will likely be interested. If they place a low value on the work, likely they will not be interested.

My wife places a high value on back-yard gardening. She has high interest and passion for the flora and fauna of the exotic jungle in our backyard. I, on the other hand, place a very low value on back-yard gardening. What do you imagine is my level of enthusiasm, when requested to report to the back yard for a task assignment?

Creating Interview Questions for a Value or Attitude

Values and attitudes are not directly observable. Direct questions about values and attitudes are seldom helpful. While it is difficult to interview for a candidate's values, it is easy to interview for a candidate's behavior connected to a value.

Barry Shamis, in his book *Hiring 3.0*, [vii] calls this his magic question. "How does a person, who has this _____ value, behave?" This magic question works to translate any soft skill, attitude or value into a behavior. Now, interview for that behavior.

Questions About Value for the Work

Some people value this work or that work. "How does a person, who values this type of work, behave?"

Tell me about a time when?
Step me through?

- Tell me about a project, in your career, that you are the most proud of?
- What was the project?
- What was the work in the project?
- What was your role?
- What was the specific work in your role?
- Tell me about another project like that?

Sense of Urgency

Some people maintain a sense of urgency, some do not. Translate the value into a behavior. "How does a person with a sense of urgency behave?

- Tell me about project where there was significant time pressure or a hard deadline?
- What was the purpose of the project?
- What created the time pressure?
- What was your role on the project?
- What did you do to keep the project on schedule?
- What did you do when the project got behind schedule?
- What did you do when the project got ahead of schedule?
- Tell me about another project like that?

Responses to these questions reveal how this candidate behaves when time is important.

Teamwork

If teamwork is a critical role requirement, translate the value into a behavior. How does a person who values teamwork behave?

- Tell me about a project where teamwork was important?
- What was the project?
- What was your role on the project?
- How many people were on the team?
- What was it, about the project that required the team to work closely together?
- What did you do to organize the team?
- When the team worked well, what were they doing?
- When the team did not work well, what were they doing?
- In your role, with the team, what did you do that improved their teamwork?
- Tell me about another project like that?

Constructing Questions for Reasonable Behavior

Reasonable behavior has two areas to explore.

- Habits
- Absence of minus "T," an extreme negative temperament

Habits

The positive side of reasonable behavior is habits. Candidates have habits that contribute to their success and habits that detract from their success. In many ways, habits spell the difference between success and failure. The same method to create questions for values can be used to create questions about habits.

Creating Questions for Habits

If a critical role requirement is frequent follow-up with teammates, that behavior, as a habit, may contribute to success in the role. The absence of that behavior, as a habit, may prove to be a weakness.

Tell me about a project when?
Step me through?

- Tell me about a project involving a number of steps where you self-performed none of the steps, but had to rely on your team members for completion?
- What was the project?
- What was the time-span of the project?
- What was your role on the project?
- How many team members on the project?
- How many milestones in the project?
- How did you organize the project with your team?
- Step me through the milestones?
- Tell me about another project like that?

In the responses to these questions, the interviewer should listen for follow-up, the quality of the follow-up, the frequency of the follow-up, the formality or informality of the follow-up.

Minus "T"

In reasonable behavior, Jaques identified what he called, minus "T." The "T" stands for temperament. Many hiring processes employ profile assessments or personality profiles to gain insight into a candidate's suitability for a role. What these profile assessments attempt to measure is the behavior connected with the candidate's temperament. In most cases, Jaques paid little attention to profiles in the normal range, but was only concerned with extreme profile results. In spite of all other positive characteristics, an extreme negative temperament will ultimately derail a candidate's effectiveness in the role.

Most of the time, behavior falls into the reasonable category. Jaques found minus "T" emerges under situations of stress.

Creating Questions for Minus T

Tell me about a time when?
Step me through?

- Tell me about a project where the client was making unreasonable demands?
- What was the project?
- What was the time-span of the project?
- What was your role on the project?
- What was the unreasonable demand?
- In your role, how did you respond to the demand?
- Tell me about another project like that?

Disagreements

- Tell me about a time, working with a group, where you disagreed with the direction of the group?
- What was the purpose of the group?
- What project were they working on?
- What was the time-span of the project?
- What was your role in the group?
- What was the disagreement about?

- How did you learn of the disagreement?
- How did you respond?
- Step me through the conversation?
- Tell me about another project like that?

Interpersonal Conflict

- Tell me about a time when you disagreed with the direction set by your manager?
- What was the project?
- What was the time-span of the project?
- Purpose of the project?
- Describe the role of your manager related to the project?
- Describe your role related to the project?
- How did you learn of the disagreement?
- How did you respond?
- Step me through the conversation?
- Tell me about another project like that?

Some profile instruments do a remarkable job of identifying how candidates respond under pressure, disagreement or conflict and have demonstrated statistical validity. While it is not advised to make hiring decisions solely based on them, profiles can help the interviewer explore areas that may have been missed.

Organizing Questions

Creating effective questions is a start, but to be truly effective, these questions have to be organized so the interviewer can clearly see the patterns of past behavior. The structure of the role description helps the interviewer organize these questions into Key Result Areas directly related to the work in the open role.

Ten Questions in each KRA

Each KRA in the role description contains tasks, activities and accountabilities that become the source for effective questions. Using the role description, it is easy to create, in each KRA, a minimum of ten written questions. If the role description contains 5-8 KRAs, that should yield a bank of 50-80 written prepared questions. This may sound like a lot of work, but a bit of practice makes this a very easy exercise.

Understand that, for each written question, the interviewer is likely to ask two clarifying or drill-down questions. This means, during a 60-90 minute interview, the interviewer may easily ask 150-240 questions.

It should become clear, now, why traditional approaches to interviews, with open-ended, hypothetical and future-based questions fail so miserably when it comes to choosing the best candidate. It should, also, become clear why it is okay that the interviewer holds stereotypes, bias and a first impression. By the conclusion of the interview, there will be 180 pieces of data to balance that bias.

Working With an Interview Team

Interview team members can be a great source of input to the hiring manager, but only if they are prepared to participate effectively. The reason most interview team members are unprepared, is the same reason most managers are unprepared. There is little work done creating the role description and most interviews are conducted on the fly, with no prepared questions.

Team Participation

Interview teams can participate at each of the preparation steps in this process. HR professionals can assist both managers and interview team members by facilitating the necessary steps. Team conversations can help define the KRAs, the tasks, activities and accountabilities in the role.

The interview team can meet together or work individually to create the prepared questions for each KRA. They can meet and decide which interview team members may focus on specific KRAs while other team members focus on others.

Defective Selection

The worst case is interview team members who take their participation casually and arrive in the interview room unprepared. Their lack of preparation will carry through the process and their influence on the final selection will likely be defective. As interview teams are put together, the manager-once-removed must insist on this process and require genuine participation.

Field Work

If you are using this book as a practical field guide, this is your opportunity to create a bank of interview questions, using the Key Result Areas in your role description for a real role in your organization. This will be most helpful if your organization is currently recruiting for this role.

Example Field Work

What follows is a report on real field work, based on this exercise, assembling a bank of interview questions in each KRA for the role of a floor supervisor.

From the role description, what is the title and purpose for this role?
Floor Supervisor, the purpose of this role is to ensure that all materials, personnel and equipment are scheduled to meet the daily, weekly and monthly production requirements dictated by the target production output list.

Who is the hiring manager?
The hiring manager is the Plant Manager

KRA#1, critical role requirements, ten questions for this KRA?
Raw Material Inventory

Critical role requirements
Maintain computerized inventory for raw materials, including receiving and stocking.

1. Tell me about the raw materials inventory you maintained?
2. How many SKUs in the inventory?

3. What were the on-hand quantities of each?
4. How did you keep track of the quantity on-hand?
5. How did you know when to re-order?
6. How many total vendors did you deal with?
7. How many vendors did you have for each SKU?
8. How was pricing for the raw materials handled for each vendor?
9. Step me through the receiving process for your three largest SKUs?
10. How were the bin locations in your warehouse organized?

KRA#2, critical role requirements, ten questions for this KRA?
Personnel Scheduling

Critical role requirements
Maintain all personnel schedules for all machines and assembly, including requests for vacation, PTO.

1. How many people on your work team?
2. How many shifts?
3. How many days per week?
4. How did you make work assignments?
5. How did you organize and communicate work assignments to the team?
6. How often did those assignments change, during the week after the schedule was posted?
7. How were those changes communicated?
8. How did you determine which team member worked on which part of production?
9. What were the specific challenges you faced in creating and executing the work schedule?
10. How did you handle vacation, PTO, holidays?

KRA#3, critical role requirements, ten questions for this KRA?
Equipment Scheduling

Critical role requirements
Maintain all machine schedules according to production requirements, including the re-scheduling of equipment that goes down.

1. How many pieces of equipment were used in the production operation?
2. Describe the heavy equipment vs the light equipment and tools?
3. Step me through how you scheduled the equipment on a weekly basis?
4. After machines were scheduled for the week, how often would that schedule change to accommodate production?
5. How did you communicate those changes to your manager and to your team?
6. Step me through your issues related to machine up-time and down-time?
7. How often did your equipment schedule change related to up-time or down-time?
8. How did you communicate those changes to your manager and to your team?
9. How did you resolve issues related to actual production vs scheduled production?
10. How did you communicate that resolution to your manager and to your team?

KRA#4, critical role requirements, ten questions for this KRA?
Production Output

Critical role requirements
Monitor production line operations, solve production line problems, and coordinate changes.

1. How many steps in the production line operation?
2. How many people on the production line, in each production cell?
3. How did you monitor production output so you could tell when things were going right and when things were going wrong?
4. What was the most severe production problem that you faced on the line?
5. How frequent did that production problem occur?
6. What was the impact to production when that problem occurred?
7. How did you gather data about that production problem?
8. How did you participate in the resolution to re-occurring production problems?
9. How did you collect data to determine actual production output on the line?
10. What reports did you publish on production output and who did you review them with?

KRA#5, critical role requirements, ten questions for this KRA?
Equipment Maintenance

Critical role requirements
Make sure all equipment is properly maintained to ensure maximum up-time and to coordinate machines offline for scheduled maintenance.

1. How many machines on the floor that required an established routine maintenance program?
2. Step me through the tracking system for routine maintenance on your major equipment?
3. Who actually completed the routine maintenance?

4. How was the quality of the routine maintenance controlled?
5. How did you control equipment taken offline for routine maintenance related to the production schedule?
6. What was the longest period where a piece of equipment was offline for maintenance?
7. Tell me about a time when there was a schedule conflict between a piece of equipment's production and its scheduled maintenance?
8. What was the life cycle of your major pieces of equipment?
9. What reports did you maintain related to life cycles of your major equipment?
10. Step me through the process for replacement of your major pieces of equipment?

KRA#6, critical role requirements, ten questions for this KRA?
Personnel and Recruiting

Critical role requirements
Participate in the hiring process. This role acts as the hiring manager for production team members.

1. How many people on your production team?
2. What was the average length of employment of your production team?
3. What was the longest tenure? shortest tenure?
4. Who created the role description for production team members?
5. What skills did you interview for?
6. What questions did you ask?
7. What other qualities are important for a production team member?
8. What questions did you ask?
9. What attitudes did you look for in candidates?
10. What questions did you ask?

KRA#5, critical role requirements, ten questions for this KRA?

Member of safety committee.

Critical Role Requirements

Be an active member of the company's safety committee.

1. Tell me about a time when you were a member of a plant safety committee?
2. What was the specific purpose of the committee?
3. Who else was a member of the committee?
4. What was your specific role on the committee?
5. What issues did the committee work on?
6. How did they resolve those issues?
7. How did the committee report on their work to management?
8. How did the committee report on their work to the production team?
9. How did the committee influence production training programs?
10. What was the one most successful issue resolved by the safety committee?

Part IV – Conducting the Interview

Candidates Have Been Coached

Most managers are unprepared and candidates have been professionally coached.

In the days before managers schedule interviews with candidates, do they role play with their interview team? Of course not. They are too busy.

Here is the bad news. Candidates are being coached. Candidates are role-playing with professional recruiters. They are preparing to beat the interviewer. They will hide critical things from the interviewer. They have selected words that will impress. The candidate will misdirect the interview to places that have nothing to do with the open role. They will deal in hypothetical examples, to say things they think the interviewer wants to hear, what they have been coached to say.

Preparation - Foundation of an Effective Interview

Susan, the hiring manager, arrived at the office, 7:45a, to take care of a few things and get ready for a candidate interview at 9:00a. A quick check of her email took twenty minutes, but that's okay, she was waiting for a pot of coffee to brew anyway. A team member stopped in to get clarification on a project that was stalled. A client phone call snatched a few more precious minutes. At 8:50a, the receptionist announced the arrival of the candidate.

Susan searched through the stack of papers on her desk, locating the candidate's resume. Luckily, she had scratched a couple of questions in the margins to make sure she asked about a specific skill required for the role. Quickly skimming the professional formatting, she set off for the conference room to meet the candidate.

Preparation Required

Susan was already behind the curve. As the interviewer, on the surface, she might appear in control, with the power in the conversation, but underneath, she surrendered to a process that failed to capture the meaningful data to make an effective decision.

Three Documents

Preparation begins in the days before the actual interview. Susan needs three central documents.

- Role description
- Printed list of questions
- Candidate resume

Role Description

The role description is the cornerstone of this process. It organizes similar tasks and activities into Key Result Areas (KRAs). The role description specifically defines the accountabilities.

Printed List of Questions

In each KRA, the task and accountabilities are translated into critical role requirements. From those critical role requirements, specific questions are created to identify the candidate's related experience and past behavior. The list contains approximately ten written prepared questions in each Key Result Area.

Candidate Resume

The candidate's resume is the third document for the interview. There are a thousand formats for a resume. Pay attention to spelling and understandability. Discount perfumed paper and fancy fonts.

Most resumes are written in reverse chronological order, most recent experience at the top. During resume review, and during the interview, start from the bottom and work up, in chronological order. During the interview, the manager is looking for patterns of learning and growth during the candidate's career experience. Patterns are difficult to see working backward through time. Start at the beginning and work forward to the present. The patterns of experience, learning and growth will be easier to see.

Before the Interview

In those few minutes prior to meeting the candidate, shut out distractions, close the door and study these three documents, a minimum of fifteen minutes. Significant time has already been spent, organizing both the role description and the list of questions, so this review period is to focus on the conversation ahead. The resume was likely reviewed several times prior to setting this appointment. This last review is to connect the role description and the questions with the data on the resume.

Your List of Questions and Taking Notes

During the interview, the primary documents are the list of questions and the candidate resume. With a list of 60 written questions and asking two clarifying questions for each written question, the interviewer will ask approximately 180 questions during the course of the interview. There will be a lot of data on the table.

Make only sparse notes on the resume. Use the question list pages for the bulk of your note-taking. Format the question list with room on the side for notes. There will be a lot of data, so, invent shorthand to record responses and create symbols to draw attention to important details.

It will be impossible to record every detail. Make essential notes that are helpful for later review. Schedule a minimum of fifteen minutes following the interview to expand the notes so they will make sense one or two days, or a week later.

Questions	Notes

Pace in the Interview

The larger the role, the more time should be reserved for the interview. Small roles may only require 20-30 minutes, but supervisory and managerial roles will require 60-90-120 minutes. Candidate selection is an important decision. Take the appropriate amount of time.

At first it may seem odd, stepping up the pace. With 60 written prepared questions and two clarifying questions for each written question, approximately 180 questions will be asked during the course of the interview. That is a lot of questions. If the interview is 60 minutes in length, that is one new question every twenty seconds. The pace of this interview is quite different.

Typical interviews have only six prepared questions. The interviewer asks a question and sits back allowing the candidate to make up stories for 2-3 minutes, before asking another question. It is no wonder, the interviewer seldom finds out what is needed. The interviewer most often finds out only what the candidate wants to tell.

Interrupting the Candidate

Candidates are used to the old pace. They practice rambling. The interviewer often has to interrupt the candidate response, so the interview can move on.

Every Question Has a Purpose

Move on. When the candidate has responded with the data needed, stop the candidate and move to the next question.

Refocus

Even with a specific question, candidates often drift into a hypothetical response.

Interviewer - "Tell me about a time when you had to work under a tight deadline?"

Candidate - "Well, when I work on tight deadlines, I always do planning."

Interviewer - "No, tell me about a specific time when you had to work under a tight deadline. You said, you worked on the ABC project, what was the deadline on that project?"

Candidate - "Oh, well, yes, there was a tight deadline."

Interviewer - "So, on the ABC project, what was the deadline?"

Candidate - "Well, inside the project, there were strict deadlines, every two weeks on Friday."

Interviewer - "Tell me about the planning you did to meet those deadlines?"

Candidate - "Oh, we didn't do any planning on *that* project. The client controlled all the steps."

When the interviewer asks specific questions about real events, the truth emerges.

Listening for Level of Work

The most difficult part of the interview is to identify a candidate's capability related to the level of work. Don't try. The effort will throw you off track. Attempting to identify a person's capability is like playing amateur psychologist. Managers may have taken a course in psychology, but most managers didn't study for it, don't have degrees in it, aren't certified in it. Do not play amateur psychologist.

Most managers, however, can spot positive behavior out in the field or on the plant floor. Most managers can spot negative behavior, and can tell the difference in a nanosecond. Interviewers should avoid playing amateur psychologist, but play to their strengths as a manager.

Do not attempt to climb inside the head of the candidate, instead, listen carefully for their behavior. Listen carefully for the level of work. Listen carefully for the length of the longest time-span task. Jaques laid the groundwork for a diagnostic interview in his *Time-span Handbook*.[viii] This interview contains ten questions, designed to reveal the level of work, calibrated by the length of the longest time-span task.

Here are the questions.
Interviewer: I want to talk about your job, your role with the company.

* Tell me, what is your job title?
* Describe, generally what you do?
* How are you given work assignments?
* How often are you given work assignments?

- When you complete a work assignment, how does your manager know?
- When you complete a work assignment, how do you know what to work on next?
- Does anyone review or inspect your work?
- How often is your work reviewed or inspected?
- Are you permitted (or directed) to continue on additional work before your current work has been reviewed?
- Do you work on multiple assignments simultaneously? Describe?

Time-Span of Discretion

These questions are specifically designed to reveal the period of time during which the team member has decision making authority, the time-span of discretion. Even Level I roles have decisions to be made. In these questions, the interviewer is listening for the period of time where the manager has specifically given authority to the team member to make those decisions.

In each question, here are the clues to listen for.

Tell me, what is your job title?
Listen for key words like
Level I - Labor, Technician, Clerical, Production
Level II – Supervisor, Coordinator
Level III - Manager, Director
Level IV - Vice President, Chief-Anything except Chief Executive.

Describe, generally what you do?
Listen for work descriptors.
Level I will indicate *individual* direct production work with short time-span tasks.

Level II will describe scheduling, coordinating, conducting frequent huddles and short meetings, to make sure production work is completed.
Level III will describe systems, sequence, analysis, cause and effect relationships.
Level IV will describe multiple systems, sub-systems and the system relationships to each other in the organization.

How are you given work assignments?

Listen for the manner in which work is assigned, whether by direct task assignment, from a schedule or list, short term goals established in a meeting or longer term goals established in a series of meetings.

How often are you given work assignments?

The frequency of *new* work assigned may indicate the start of time-span tasks.

When you complete a work assignment, how does your manager know?

This question may help establish the end of time-span tasks.

When you complete a work assignment, how do you know what to work on next?

This question helps to see sequenced work inside a longer project. Does the team member decide what to work on next, or does activity stop, waiting on further instructions from the manager? This helps pinpoint the time-span of discretion for the team member.

Does anyone review or inspect your work?

Often, the end of a task is not clearly defined by the manager. Work inspection (for quality, completeness) may mark the end of a time-span task.

How often is your work reviewed or inspected?
The frequency of work review may also indicate the time-span of discretion of the team member. Is work output reviewed daily, weekly, monthly, quarterly?

Are you permitted (or directed) to continue on additional work before your current work has been reviewed?
Sometimes, a review point, or lack of a review point, may be a false indicator for the end of the task. This question is to probe the candidate for details to more clearly establish the length of the task.

Do you work on multiple assignments simultaneously? Describe?
This question helps to clarify simultaneous work. The purpose of all of these questions is to establish the longest time-span task in the role.

Four Illustrative Interviews

Here are four illustrative interviews. In each interview, listen for the level of work. Following each interview, identify the length of the longest time-span task and identify the level of work.

Ringo's Interview

I want to talk about your job, your role with the company. Tell me, what is your job title?
Carpenter

Describe, generally what you do?
Finish-work, I am on the installation crew. We get the cabinets in place and nail in the trim.

How are you given work assignments?
In the morning, we get together, count the boxes to be installed, eyeball our raw millwork, to make sure we have enough, then get to it. We have drawings taped to the wall in each room so we know where things go.

How often are you given work assignments?
We have two meetings a day. The morning meeting and then one in the afternoon to clue us in on the following day. Sometimes we move from one job, one day, to another job, the next day.

When you complete a work assignment, how does your manager know?

Generally, our crew chief is walking the job from room to room, so he knows pretty close. We're in constant touch.

When you complete a work assignment, how do you know what to work on next?
Most of the time, if it looks like we will finish a room or a wing in the middle of the day, we will schedule a mid-day meeting. The crew chief doesn't want us to get the specs for two different setups mixed up.

Does anyone review or inspect your work?
Each crew has a crew chief.

How often is your work reviewed or inspected?
Our crew chief seems to constantly inspect. He comes behind, verifies a few measurements, looks at the finish-work. He doesn't want us to get too far ahead in case we have to come back and fix something.

Are you permitted (or directed) to continue on additional work before your current work has been reviewed?
We can work ahead, as long as it's in the same room or wing, so we don't get too far away. And we generally don't strike our ladders and tool boxes until we've been given the all clear to move on.

Do you work on multiple assignments simultaneously? Describe?
We could work on installing cabinets and do trim work during the same morning, it has more to do with proximity than anything else.

Your Judgment –

Level of Work in Current Role _____
Clues _____

Debriefing Ringo's Interview

This is clearly a Level I role focused on *individual* direct output. The job title is that of a technician. The time-span of discretion is described as two days, where the crew meets with their manager to talk about work the following day. So, while they are working on one day, they may anticipate setup requirements for the next day.

George's Interview

I want to talk about your job, your role with the company. Tell me, what is your job title?
Crew Chief

Describe, generally what you do?
I work on-site with the installation crews. Depending on the project, I may actually be running more than one crew, just depends. My crews do the installation of pre-manufactured cabinets, we manufacture those back at the shop.

How are you given work assignments?
I meet with the Ops guys back at the shop. My manager works pretty close with the project managers, mainly handling logistics and scheduling.

How often are you given work assignments?
We meet once a week to review the installations on the board for that week. We review all the details, you know, how many guys we will need, what cabinets are ready to roll, and what trim pieces are ready. Usually, we try to make it all in one trip, reduce travel time between the shop and the site. At that same meeting, we also look at two more weeks after this week. We don't hit all the details, but just so I can be thinking about what's coming up. I might have to shift a crew around if a project gets delayed. Or, I might be able to get a jump ahead on a project.

When you complete a work assignment, how does your manager know?
We are all on push-to-talk radios. Everybody is up to date, everybody knows

where we are, in real time. That way, we can respond fast if there is a problem, or maybe we get ahead on a project.

When you complete a work assignment, how do you know what to work on next?

Well, that's why we look ahead three to four weeks, you know, not in detail. But, I have a good idea what's coming up. If we get finished early, I usually always have a game plan going. Of course, most of the time, it is working-in extra stuff that wasn't on the schedule. But here's where the job really gets tricky. We get a long range schedule that goes out three months. Sometimes, I look at that schedule and realize I have to hire a couple of more people, or if we are not busy, I may have to lay off a couple of people. Doing the work is easy, but looking that far ahead, I really have to think.

Does anyone review or inspect your work?

I am usually the field inspector on workmanship. The stuff my manager talks to me about is how much we actually get done according to the schedule that was laid out by the project manager. The PMs have a pretty good idea what it takes to complete different types of work, so we try to stick pretty close to their schedule. My manager talks to me about production, overtime, making sure we have the right materials on the job. It's also my job to coordinate with other trades, the construction manager from the General Contractor, heck, sometimes, even the owner shows up. I have to know enough about what is going on to answer their questions about schedule changes and change orders.

How often is your work reviewed or inspected?
I meet with my manager once a week for scheduling, but once a month we sit down and just take a look at the overall picture. What jobs are where. We also do a post mortem after we finish a project to find out where we did well and where we need to improve for the next project. Those post mortems are done at the end of most big projects or even big phases of huge projects, could be every three to four months.

Are you permitted (or directed) to continue on additional work before your current work has been reviewed?
Oh, yeah. The show must go on. Except where there is a real time emergency, most of the things we talk about are looking forward to the next job. You know, lessons learned. Only occasionally do we get caught midstream and have to make a major adjustment.

Do you work on multiple assignments simultaneously? Describe?
Sure, for those projects which have different kinds of things going on. For example, we may be installing cabinetry in one part of a building, and doing finish work on a wooden bar and cherry wood molding in another part of the building.

Your Judgment –

Level of Work in Current Role _____
Clues _____

Debriefing George's Interview

This is a Level II role focused on much more than *individual* direct output. The purpose of this role is to coordinate people, equipment and materials. A primary tool for this role is a project schedule.

Post mortems on projects extend beyond the three month cutoff for Level I roles. Three month look-aheads are required for personnel recruiting. The candidate reveals the relative ease of short term scheduling but describes difficulty with the longer term planning, where he really has to think.

A more specific calibration of this level of work would be Low Level II, time-span between 3-6 months.

Paul's Interview

I want to talk about your job, your role with the company. Tell me, what is your job title?
Construction Manager

Describe, generally what you do?
I meet with the Project Managers to make sure their projects are being completed on schedule. They each have individual projects happening. I bring it all together from a logistics and scheduling point of view.

How are you given work assignments?
I meet with the PMs on a weekly basis, just to catch up on progress completed the prior week and update them on the logistics for this week. I have to coordinate with our manufacturing shop to make sure the manufactured cabinets and installation components are all coming out to staging at the right time to be installed.

How often are you given work assignments?
Well, even though we meet on a weekly basis, I am really trying to run, believe or not, one year ahead of schedule. I use a project management software to book out the jobs based on various schedules and the contracts. It's not really my job to dissect everything, but I do it anyway, just to double-check, make sure no one is asking for the impossible. It's only when I plan out a year, especially for some of our big jobs, that I can work in all the smaller jobs. Things get very fluid at times. It's easy to get in the weeds.

When you complete a work assignment, how does your manager know?

At each weekly meeting, we produce a short set of minutes that logs progress. That is all entered in our project management software that our COO has access to. Believe me, he knows. We may not talk about it, but he knows.

When you complete a work assignment, how do you know what to work on next?

It's pretty well all laid out. I know from experience what all the next steps are. Though our projects are complicated, they have distinct phases to them. So, no one really tells me what I have to do next.

Does anyone review or inspect your work?

The COO and I work pretty close together, even though we may not talk all that much. Our control systems are centered around the software. Each quarter, we sit down and take a look at the PM schedules to complete, take a look at the budgets to see where we are. I am doing a good job when everyone's expectations are in line with reality.

How often is your work reviewed or inspected?

Well, in addition to the quarterly meetings, we sit down and do a post mortem on each project. Some of our projects take a year to complete, sometimes longer with change orders or a complete change in scope of work.

Are you permitted (or directed) to continue on additional work before your current work has been reviewed?

Absolutely, we always have projects happening at the same time. We don't stop just because we haven't had a post mortem.

Do you work on multiple assignments simultaneously? Describe?
Generally, we have, maybe thirty jobs going in one stage or another. Now, some of them are small, maybe take only 2-3 weeks to complete, but we always have two or three major jobs, and once a year, we usually get "THE BIG ONE." That one will take at least a year to complete.

Your Judgment –

Level of Work in Current Role _____
Clues _____

Debriefing Paul's Interview
This has the appearance of a scheduling role, but the time-span reveals more complexity than George's scheduling role. The time-span of the scheduling extends beyond one year and requires project management software to be effective.

The coordination of elements is also more complex, not just coordinating a single crew, but the output of different work cells. Scheduling even the small stuff requires a 12 month look ahead to fit everything in.

Paul describes his thinking as dissecting. He takes elements apart to more clearly understand the cause and effect elements that occur inside the work. This would be a clue toward analysis, a predictable characteristic of Level III problem solving. Level of work is low Level III, longest time-span task, 12-13 months.

John's Interview

I want to talk about your job, your role with the company. Tell me, what is your job title?
> COO

Describe, generally what you do?
> I am in charge of all operations, from manufacturing, to installation, to plant facilities, vehicles, machinery, space requirements. I have both a capital budget and project budgets to work with. It's quite a big job.

How are you given work assignments?
> I meet with the CEO, formally, once a month, informally, quite often. I'm not sure if I actually get assignments, it's more like initiatives.

How often are you given work assignments?
> We formulate these initiatives on an annual basis, though we may modify them quarterly, we always have a solid game plan every January.

When you complete a work assignment, how does your manager know?
> The work is never done. Of course, we usually always have a big project in house. Logistically, it takes more than a year to complete, but there is a lot more that goes into it, you know, even before mobilization and there is even work after the punch list is completed.

When you complete a work assignment, how do you know what to work on next?

I can go to one of two places. Like I said, we always have the annual game plan, but we also have a rolling plan that goes out for three years. I am always thinking about what we need to be doing now that will get us in the right position for what we think will happen three years from now.

Does anyone review or inspect your work?

We look at financial performance once a month, but the annual game plan, we take two days each quarter to review. We may make adjustments and always formulate our robust next steps.

How often is your work reviewed or inspected?

In addition to the monthly and quarterly meetings, we do a thorough shakedown every December. That gives us an opportunity to clarify our last operating plan and also look forward at our three-year rolling plan.

Are you permitted (or directed) to continue on additional work before your current work has been reviewed?

As long as it is consistent with our operating plan, or conceptually consistent with our three-year plan. Of course, the three-year plan is more conceptual.

Do you work on multiple assignments simultaneously? Describe?

I am always working on multiple things, but it is only because I have talented managers underneath me that work diligently at the nuts and bolts of our operations.

Your Judgment –

Level of Work in Current Role _____
Clues _____

Debriefing John's Interview
The title of COO points toward Level IV. Task assignments do not come from specific directives, but from initiatives in annual planning documents. The time-span of discretion is extended further by reference to a rolling three year plan. It would be valuable to confirm John's active participation in the preparation of that three year plan, but with sufficient evidence, the conclusion of a Level IV role is certain.

His description that the "work is never done" is consistent with Level IV. It takes a very long time to gain job satisfaction from a project that takes 2-5 years to complete. And the credit always goes to the talented team, because the tangible work product experienced by the customer is seldom connected to the foresight of a manager who, three years ago, arranged for the capital equipment to do the job.

It's All About the Work

In each debrief, calibrating capability was centered on the level of work. Focus on the work. Managers are experts about the work. Don't play amateur psychologist.

Decision Matrix

With several candidates, even with 2-3 good candidates, it is often tough to make a decision. This decision model is a variation of a traditional model called absolutes-and-desirables, or needs-and-wants. This model specifies what is absolutely necessary, and what would be desirable to have in the successful candidate.

It is a simple model. Down the side, grouped by Key Result Areas (KRAs) are the critical role requirements. Across the top are the candidates. The interviewer can use any coding system to score the candidates (A-B-C-F), (plus/minus), (0-10). The coding is not intended to be added up at the end. The coding is to help organize and remember the differences between candidates.

This decision model is helpful, helping the manager remember things forgotten. Immediately following the interview, in addition to fleshing out the interview notes, each member of the interview team should record their judgments for each of the critical role requirements in their copy of the decision matrix.

Critical Role Requirements	Candidate A	Candidate B	Candidate C
Req #1			
Req #2			
Req #3			
Req #4			
Req #5			
Req #6			
Req #7			

Hiring Manager Makes the Decision

The decision matrix is a tool for capturing detailed judgments for each of the critical role requirements. It is important to note that each interview team member may score things differently. Differences of opinion create a good place for team discussion.

While it is helpful for the interview team to debrief and calibrate responses, the final hiring decision is still in the hands of the hiring manager. The decision matrix organizes the data collected about each candidate and provides some logic for making the decision.

Working With an Interview Team

Interview teams have become popular and for good reason. The space of 60-90 minutes is a short time to make such an important decision. Multiple interviews create additional perspectives and allow for specific questions in technical areas, all providing important data for the hiring manager.

The problem with most interview teams is the lack of discipline. Casual participation can create as many problems as helpful points of view. Voices from the interview team all sound equal, though some interviews may have been conducted without proper preparation.

Interview teams can help organize the role description and create the interview questions. Not only does it make the process more effective, it splits up the work.

In separate interviews, it is not necessary that each interviewer ask identical questions. Indeed, separate interviews may focus on different technical areas and critical role requirements.

No Group Interviews

There has been a move, by some, toward group interviewing. Group interviews create dynamics which may be counterproductive, on both candidate and interviewer. The purpose of the interview is to gather discrete pieces of data about experience related to critical role requirements. Multiple people asking related and unrelated questions, introduces stress and chaos into the interview. This may not allow the candidate to calmly remember situations.

Unconsciously, in a group interview, team members have an impact on each other. One clouds the judgment of the other. Better to have interviewers ask their own questions, without the influence of other interview team members.

Who is Accountable for the Decision?

With the benefits of an interview team, the selection decision still rests with the hiring manager. No one else can make the call. It is only the hiring manager who will be accountable for the output of the team member. The hiring manager must have minimum veto authority.

Field Work

If you are using this book as a practical field guide, this is an opportunity to conduct an interview, using the role description and list of questions you created. If you have an external candidate ready to interview, that would certainly make a good subject. However, it is more likely that you will "practice" on an internal team member.

Internal team members, who have experience related to the role, make perfect subjects for practice. In most cases, I prefer that you practice on an internal team member before you practice on real candidates. This will be most helpful if your organization is currently recruiting for this role.

Set aside 30-60 minutes to conduct the interview. You will be asking questions and taking notes during the interview. Following the interview, do a self-debrief to flesh out your notes and complete the decision matrix.

Self-Debrief

In your self-debrief, here are some questions to consider.

- In the interview you conducted, what was the title and purpose of the role?
- Describe your list of questions, how were they organized, how many questions in total?
- Describe how many of your written questions you asked during the interview and how many clarifying questions you created during the interview?
- How long was your interview? Describe the pace of your questions in this interview compared to the pace of your questions in prior interviews?
- At the end of this interview, describe the quality of the data collected compared with prior interviews?
- Describe the notes you took during this interview (including the self-debrief) compared to notes you took in prior interviews?
- Describe how the decision matrix will help you make the selection decision in the future?
- What was the best idea or discovery (about interviewing) you made during this exercise?

Example Debrief

Here is an example of a real debrief, from a manager following the Hiring Talent process.

In the interview you conducted, what was the title and purpose of the role?
Floor Supervisor, the purpose of this role is to ensure that all materials, personnel and equipment are scheduled to meet the daily, weekly and monthly production requirements dictated by the target production output list.

Describe your list of written questions, how were they organized, how many questions in total?
I had a total of 70 questions. I had six KRAs, with ten questions apiece and ten additional questions.

Describe how many of your written questions you asked during the interview and how many clarifying questions you created during the interview?
During the interview, I only asked 30 of the written questions, but I probably asked twice that many questions that I made up on-the-fly. With one written question, it was very easy to create 2-3 more questions to clarify the responses.

How long was your interview? Describe the pace of your questions in this interview compared to the pace of your questions in prior interviews?
My interview was about 40 minutes long. I probably asked 80-90 questions, which means, on average, one new question every thirty seconds. It seemed weird to ask that many

questions, but it was easier than I thought it would be.

At the end of this interview, describe the quality of the data collected compared with prior interviews?
I never got so much information out of an interview. Before, most of the time, at the end of an interview, I would still be asking myself if I thought the candidate could be successful. But I could never pinpoint why I felt one way or the other.

Describe the notes you took during this interview (including the self-debrief) compared to notes you took in prior interviews?
I quickly developed some shorthand, mainly check marks, happy and sad faces. During the interview, it was really hard to take detailed notes, but I took enough to reconstruct things once the interview was over. In prior interviews, I would make notes on the resume. This means, my notes explained their resume, but not whether I thought they would be able to do the job.

Describe how the decision matrix helped you make the selection decision?
The decision matrix helped record my reaction to the specific role requirements. This was extremely helpful in remembering each candidate's strengths and weaknesses. The decision jumped off the page.

What was the best idea or discovery (about interviewing) you made during this exercise?
This is completely different from any interview I have ever conducted. It was funny how, now, I could tell when the candidate was making up an answer because he thought it would sound good

to me. It was only when I forced the candidate to think about a specific example that the truth came out.

Part V – Details, Details

The Other Steps

There are four big steps where most interviews go wrong, but in between, are other steps with their own problems.

Step by Step

- Evaluate the necessity for the position
- **Identify the level of work (Part I)**
- **Organize the role description (Part II)**
- Write the job posting
- **Create a bank of interview questions (Part III)**
- Source candidates
- Resume intake and sorting
- Telephone screens
- Telephone interview (including Skype)
- **Conduct the face-to-face interview (Part IV)**
- Permissions and releases
- Behavioral assessments
- Background checks
- Reference checks
- Drug screen
- Selection process
- Make the offer
- Orientation
- Training
- Evaluation period

Necessity for the Position

No company purchases a piece of equipment or a tool that is not necessary. Yet, companies willingly hire people to play roles that are ill defined in scope and purpose. Is this role necessary? Does this role truly support the overarching vision and mission of the company, the department and this specific work team? What value will this position bring to the overall capacity and throughput of the team? Is the expense for this resource within the budget? Does the value of this role net a return to the company?

In short, is this role necessary?

This question is where the hiring process begins. Significant discussion between the manager and the manager-once-removed should surface appropriate arguments and criteria for this decision.

Write the Job Posting

The job posting is different from the role description. Its first purpose is to attract the candidates you want. The second purpose is to discourage candidates that will waste your time. It is a fine line, pulling in the people you want, pushing away the people you don't want.

Think from the mind of the candidate. What would a candidate want to find in the role you have open? What would a candidate want to find, working for a company like yours? What, about your company, makes it a great place to work?

Source Candidates

Candidates are fluid. They move in and out of the job market, hundreds of thousands, each and every day. They congregate in popular places, on job boards, in national databases and now, in social media. You can pull candidates toward you or you can search them out.

Paid job boards, classified advertising, in print and internet, pull candidates toward you. But while the internet has made your reach longer and in many cases less expensive, your casting net will bring in all kinds of candidates, perhaps more than you can handle. Parsing those submittals requires focused review time and a little technology. Key word searches may help narrow the field, bringing more relevant candidates to the top of the list.

The best candidates are not looking for work and are not trolling job boards. Key word searches on LinkedIn and Facebook may produce a robust list that can be filtered by geography or specialty. Even if you do not move them into your current candidate pool, those connections can be valuable for future searches.

Telephone Screens

The telephone screen has a simple purpose, with a large payoff. It answers this question, "Do I want to spend more time with this candidate?" Effective use of the telephone screen can eliminate many hours of fruitless interview time.

Select a handful of deal-breaker questions, non-negotiable absolutes. This is a qualifying step to narrow the field of candidates. Prepare two or three questions related to the level of work to produce a higher likelihood of viable candidates.

This telephone screen is short, 3-5 minutes, designed to identify those candidates to move to the next step. If the candidate does not qualify, the telephone screen allows the interviewer to quickly terminate the process. Tell candidates up-front that the length of the call will be short and contain only a few basic questions. Successful candidates can be moved to the next step.

Telephone Interviews

Before a face-to-face interview, conduct a telephone interview. This is a longer format interview, containing many of the same questions in a face-to-face interview, but without the expense of candidate travel.

If the candidate and the interviewer are both technically adept, this interview can be conducted via an internet video connection (Skype, Facetime, Go To Meeting).

More on Behavioral Assessments

Behavioral assessments are known by many names – personality profiles, personality tests, predictive tests. These instruments require a candidate to respond to a computerized list of choices or questions. Based on the responses, the test will produce a report about the subject. These tests are very popular in recruiting circles and a windfall for consultants.

Over the decades, these instruments have achieved reasonable statistical validation. Assessments can be most helpful in discovering areas for interview questions which might have been missed. They can uncover pressure points and provide insights for advanced second and third round interviews. But while an assessment can be a useful tool, it is not a substitute for a solid interview process.

Reference Checks

Unless the reference is a personal friend of the candidate, most avoid this conversation. The reference wants to avoid making a public judgment about a former employee.

Your mother taught, that if you don't have anything good to say about someone, don't say anything at all.

"Good morning, Mr. Jones. Thank you for taking my call. As you know, our company is interviewing Jim Smith for the role of supervisor. The purpose of my call is to confirm some of the facts he provided to us related to his employment with your company."

This language is specific to establish an agreement with the reference that the conversation will be about facts. Avoid the impression that there is a search for "dirt" on the candidate. If the interview process has been fact based, there should be plenty of facts to confirm.

The Compensation Question

At some point, it is helpful to understand the compensation history of our top candidates. Compensation is an indicator, if only approximate, of the level of work in the candidate's former position. Companies rarely calibrate their compensation packages with level of work, but it is still an indicator.

The subject of compensation pre-maturely dredges up all the qualities of a negotiation. On the subject of compensation, both the candidate and interviewer go on full alert.

From the interviewer's perspective, it's just another data point, but unless the question is carefully constructed, the response to the compensation question escapes the truth. Base salary is inflated by bonuses, car allowance, cell phone allowance, the value of health insurance and the raise that was promised the following year.

The truth is important. Stick to the facts.

"If I were to ask you for a copy of your W-2 (US employment form) from last year what would be the number in the box called wages?"

Carefully, write down that number in your notes.

Back to Compensation and Level of Work

Companies that have calibrated the level of work in each role, already have a specific idea of the compensation range in each level. Level of work provides a structure that supports pay-banding.

Pay-banding establishes the upper and lower limits in a level of work. From there, the manager has appropriate discretion inside each level for merit increases over time as the person matures and the level of work in the role is increased. The model below shows (18) pay bands in each level of work.

For companies who have looked at pay banding associated with levels of work, most of the mystery of compensation disappears.

Pay Banding Detail		
Level of Work	Upper Limit	Pay Band #18
		Pay Band #17
		Pay Band #16
		Pay Band #15
		Pay Band #14
		Pay Band #13
		Pay Band #12
		Pay Band #11
		Pay Band #10
		Pay Band #9
		Pay Band #8
		Pay Band #7
		Pay Band #6
		Pay Band #5
		Pay Band #4
		Pay Band #3
	Lower Limit	Pay Band #2
		Pay Band #1

Final Thoughts

Building Blocks

Hiring Talent consists of four major building blocks. There is effort required, but the process is not difficult.

- Identify the level of work
- Organize the role description
- Create a bank of interview questions
- Conduct an effective interview

Practice

Hiring Talent is a skill that requires practice. The first interview may feel choppy or difficult. Role-play with internal team members. Practice with candidates you do not intend to hire. Mastery takes practice.

What's Stopping You

Time, I need someone in the role, now.
Time, there are too many other things I have to manage.
Time, preparation is time consuming, and I have too much other work.

You do not have the time? Or, this is not a high enough priority?

It's Your Decision

Most excuses are not real reasons, just an excuse that you believe. How you go about Hiring Talent is your decision. What are you going to do?

Hiring Talent Workshop

Hiring Talent is a skill that requires practice. Mastery takes practice.

Much of the practice of Hiring Talent is written, organizing a role description and assembling a bank of interview questions. To help managers practice, I created an online course. There is work involved, but, this work is the critical difference in conducting an effective interview.

If you are serious about applying the principles in this book, visit www.hiringtalent.com. There is more information about the program and how to register. I look forward to seeing you online.

Additional Reading

It's All About Work, Organizing Your Company to Get Work Done. Stephen Clement and Chris Clement. Organizational Design Publishing. 2013.

Hiring 3.0, New Rules for the New Economy. Barry Shamis. 2010.

Requisite Organization. Elliott Jaques. Cason Hall and Co. Publishers. 1989, 1996, 1998, 2006.

Social Power and the CEO. Elliott Jaques. Quorum Books. 2002.

Human Capability. Elliott Jaques and Kathryn Cason. Cason Hall and Co. Publishers. 1994.

Executive Leadership. Elliott Jaques and Stephen Clement. Blackwell Publishers. 1991.

The Fifth Discipline. Peter Senge. Currency Doubleday. 1990.

Time-Span Handbook. Elliott Jaques. Available edition, Cason Hall Publishers. 1998. Original edition, Heinemann Educational Books, Ltd, UK. 1964.

Index

Endnotes

[i] Elliott Jaques, *Requisite Organization, A Total System for Effective Managerial Organization and Managerial Leadership for the 21st Century*, 2nd edition, revised. 2006. Cason Hall Publishers.

[ii] Jerry Harvey, *How Come Every Time I Get Stabbed in the Back, My Fingerprints Are on the Knife.* 1999. Jossey-Bass.

[iii] Elliott Jaques, *Requisite Organization, A Total System for Effective Managerial Organization and Managerial Leadership for the 21st Century*, 2nd edition, revised. 2006. Cason Hall Publishers.

[iv] Elliott Jaques, *Social Power and the CEO, Leadership and Trust in a Sustainable Free Enterprise System.* 2002. Quorum Books.

[v] Peter Senge, *The Fifth Discipline.* 1990. Currency Doubleday, p 79.

[vi] Barry Shamis, *Hiring 3.0.* 2010, p 76.

[vii] Barry Shamis, *Hiring 3.0.* 2010, p 56.

[viii] Elliott Jaques, *Time-Span Handbook.* Available edition. 1998. Cason Hall Publishers. Original edition, 1964. Heinemann Educational Books, Ltd. UK.